Mattoon

NORMAN THOMAS

THE Test

OF Freedom

NEW YORK

W·W·NORTON & COMPANY·INC.

323.44

PRINTED IN THE UNITED STATES OF AMERICA
FOR THE PUBLISHERS BY THE VAIL-BALLOU PRESS

Contents

5

Preface

THIS BOOK will speak for itself or it will not speak at all. However, I have inserted in the text references to sources of fuller treatment of several matters, since it has been my purpose to keep my own discussion of the somewhat voluminous material as brief and nontechnical as possible. I am unusually grateful to the authors whom I quote, and I owe thanks also to more persons than I remember by name, who, in oral or written discussion, have contributed to my grasp of the problem.

My special thanks are due to Sidney Hook for his logical development of the difference between heresy and conspiracy, and to the American Civil Liberties Union staff for helpful information. I am indebted to my secretary, Stephen Siteman, for more than routine clerical assistance, and to Maurice Goldbloom for reading my manuscript and offering valuable suggestions.

Nothing in the text of this book refers to any event since the middle of September, 1953. But one event is of such importance as to justify the use of this preface for comment. In November, Attorney General Brownell raised the ghost of Harry Dexter White. In the process he fed the fires of McCarthyism, and with Democratic as well as Republican help, snarled issues both of liberty and security in the toils of partisan politics. Mr. Brownell is an intelligent man, an able lawyer who has shown some regard for civil liberty. Assuredly he is aware of the climate in which communism was considered by Republicans (for instance, Wendell Willkie and General Eisenhower) as well as by Democrats in the years 1941–1947. White's conduct has properly been aired and was generally accepted as an example of communist espionage.

When the Attorney General learned that President Truman had kept Mr. White in high office after his loyalty had been seriously questioned by FBI reports placed in his hands, he would have been justified in digging up the past only if thereby he could bring to justice guilty men now living, or if he could learn how better to protect the Eisenhower administration from interpenetration and espionage. In that case, consideration for American prestige abroad, regard for the presidential office, and respect for Mr. Truman's unquestionable loyalty and international leadership in the struggle against communism should have led him first to take up the matter quietly with the former president. Instead, in language that seemed to reflect on Harry Truman's loyalty as well as his judgment, before a businessmen's lunch club in the heart of Colonel McCormick's Chicagoland, Mr. Brownell launched his charges. Whatever Mr. Brownell's intentions, his timing and the subsequent conduct of Republican spokesmen suggested an avid desire to give the Republicans a popular issue and reverse the drift toward the Democrats of which the elections on November 3 gave some indication.

The Brownell speech touched off a chain reaction of blunders—or worse. Chairman Velde rushed into the limelight with his impudent subpoena to an ex-president. President Eisenhower deplored the subpoena, but revealed to his press conference that he had given the Attorney General the green light without knowing what was involved. Mr. Truman made hasty denials which later he had to correct. Prominent Democrats hinted that Mr. Truman had kept White in office as bait for the spy ring. By the suggestion they, in effect, joined Mr. Brownell in dragging J. Edgar Hoover into the picture. In his speech to the nation over radio and TV, a speech with passages of genuine eloquence and power, Mr. Truman, without mentioning Hoover, said that after conference with Fred Vinson, then Secretary of the Treasury—and later, until his death, Chief Justice of the United States—he had indeed decided to keep White in office in order the better to watch him and other suspects. His speech suggested a good many questions which were not satisfactorily answered, and his attack on McCarthy and McCarthyism gave the Senator a chance to get equivalent time for a national broadcast in which he made the most of these unanswered questions.

But the deeper significance of the Grand Inquisitor's speech was its scarcely concealed drive against Eisenhower rather than Truman. He attacked his own party's administration for keeping John P. Davies in the diplomatic service and characteristically revived charges which Mr. Davies had answered to the satisfaction of two loyalty boards and his present superiors, including Bedell Smith, but which as an officer in our foreign service he could not answer over the air.

The Senator offered himself as the real Republican leader by attacking the President's foreign policy, by repudiating the President's expressed hope that communist interpenetration would not be an issue in the congressional elections of 1954, and by declaring: "Republican control of the Senate determines whether I shall continue as chairman of the investigating committee."

Meanwhile, Mr. Hoover had appeared before the Jenner Committee to recount the number of reports the FBI had made questioning the loyalty of Harry White and others, and his disapproval of the way President Truman had handled the case. (FBI charges admittedly fell short of completely legal proof of guilt.)

In the whole mess an ominous precedent has been set by dragging in the FBI, as not only an investigatory but a quasi-policymaking agency. The latter is not the function of the police, least of all the secret police, and the release of police reports against men living or dead, under circumstances wherein the accusation becomes, or seems to become, a final judgment, bodes no good to the defense either of our individual liberty or our national security. In the White case and in its aftermath, both liberty and security have been impaired by involving them so deeply in partisan politics.

—Norman Thomas

November 30, 1953

THE Test
OF Freedom

I.

Introducing the Subject and the Author

NOTHING IS more nearly universal in our America than the lip service paid by writers and speakers to the Bill of Rights. Nevertheless, a survey by the National Opinion Research Center in 1946, a year when civil liberties were well protected, showed that only 21 per cent of the people "gave responses indicating a reasonably accurate idea of the first ten amendments to the Constitution." And a high percentage of those who were ignorant showed disbelief in the basic rights which it defends.

The reason for ignorance was not, therefore, the fact that our liberties are so well established that we do not need to concern ourselves with constitutional guarantees of them. On the contrary, there has probably never been a time in our history when they were the subject of more

13

widespread and anxious concern than today. Yet civil liberties remain, as they were in the days of Thomas Jefferson himself, the active concern of a minority rather than a majority of the population. And while that vital minority is substantially united in praise of the Bill of Rights, strengthened by the Thirteenth, Fourteenth, and Fifteenth Amendments to the Constitution, there are wide differences of opinion in its ranks concerning the application of libertarian principles to devotees of totalitarianism, fascist or communist. These differences run the gamut from denial of any protection of civil liberty to those who in power would deny all liberty, to insistence that fascists and communists should have all the freedoms of speech and association enjoyed by other Americans. The controversy is the sharper because it takes place in the intellectual and emotional atmosphere of the cold war, in which the principal antagonists, our own country and the Soviet Union, represent the opposing ideologies of democracy and totalitarianism. What we popularly call McCarthyism is an ugly manifestation of American reaction to the troublesome situation. How immensely damaging McCarthyism is, not only at home but to our leadership and prestige abroad and the morale of our foreign service, I learned firsthand in Europe and North Africa in the summer of 1953.

It is the application of Jeffersonian principles of freedom of speech, the press and association, and of the right of every individual to protection by due process of law, that form the subject of this inquiry. We may as its result be better able to understand and oppose both McCarthyism and communism.

It will be observed that I am concerned with only one section of the whole area of civil liberty in our complex society. I shall not discuss, except incidentally, such important matters as the equality of right of all Americans regardless of race, creed, color, or national origin; or new aspects of the relation of church and state with regard to education and legislation; or the right of the people not only to speak but to hear, that is to learn the facts upon correct knowledge of which democracy depends; or the problems raised by the growth and power of strong, firmly disciplined unions in relation to the rights not only of consumers but of their own individual members.

I should, however, like to preface my present inquiry by bearing testimony to the growth of the American conscience during the years of my adult life in the field of what we now call civil rights. It has been the single most encouraging moral symptom in American society. We have a long way to go before we end racial discrimination once and for all, but the progress made strengthens my faith, even in moments of depression, that an appeal to the American conscience and intelligence is by no means wasted effort, doomed only to frustration.

In the whole field of civil liberty, above all in the area to be explored, unnecessary trouble results from our neglect of history and our tendency to use words and slogans in a vacuum apart from reality. We revere or deprecate

Jeffersonian principles without bothering to understand their origin or their role in our history. We try to dogmatize on the rights of communists on the basis, let us say, of the First Amendment without careful inquiry into the nature of communism. Therefore, before trying to set forth my convictions on such contentious matters as the right of communists to stay out of jail, or to set up their own party, or to hold civil service positions, or to teach in our schools, I shall examine briefly the Jeffersonian principles and their working through more than a century and a half of our history. I shall then turn to a discussion of the nature of communism and the peculiar problem it presents.

But first let me present my own credentials. There is no such thing as absolute objectivity where human relations are concerned. The investigator or the author is himself part of the scene which he studies and about which he writes. For his own self he cherishes above all other rights "the right to know, to utter and to argue freely according to conscience," or else he finds his chief support in external authority. His opinions on civil liberty must be affected by his own estimate of values.

As for myself, I was born into something of a non-conformist tradition. Heretics and dissenters ranked high among my youthful heroes. Work in a miserably poor tenement region of New York and the coming of World War I made me an ardent civil libertarian before they made me a socialist. Indeed, I turned to democratic socialism because

I saw in it a basis for freedom which the acquisitive society did not provide. (This, be it remembered, was in the days before Republican orators and the advertising agencies of great corporations had discovered that freedom was a by-product of the profit system, destroyed or sorely impaired by high income taxes, TVA, and other oppressions of "creeping" socialism.)

In World War I I became a pacifist on religious grounds—a position which I was constrained later to abandon. But on political grounds also I felt and said that it was America's business to keep out of the war and use her enormous moral and economic strength for a negotiated peace. I still think that that position was sound; that much of the world's tragic suffering might have been avoided, and today's likelihood of World War III lessened, if European socialists in 1914 or Woodrow Wilson in 1917 had preserved or won "peace without victory."

Such convictions as I have avowed came to be regarded by the Wilson administration, and most vocal public opinion, as treasonable or at least seditious. It was, therefore, in part self-interest that made me one of the group which under Roger Baldwin's active leadership formed the Civil Liberties Bureau, an organization which later grew into the American Civil Liberties Union. In varying degrees we of the Bureau ourselves suffered at the strong hand of the state, but we were able to render some service as time went on to the thousands of victims of what a recent histo-

rian has called Mitchell Palmer's "obscene anti-red raids."
And we avowed champions of civil liberties contributed
our bit to the return of the country to sanity.

In the twenties and thirties I still had something of a
personal interest in the defense of civil liberties. Socialism
wasn't exactly popular with anti-red crusaders, and in those
years, as late as 1937, to insist on the right of workers to organize or strike was often to invite arrest or mob violence.
I have had personal experience with both, but in those
tests we won victories for liberty.

In the various struggles in which I was most interested,
communism was not yet an issue, or was only indirectly
an issue. The victims in Wilson's administration were anarchists, socialists, wobblies (members of the IWW), often
innocent bystanders. Sacco and Vanzetti weren't communists or defended primarily by communists. (The latter
raised money for their party under the pretext of using it
for Sacco and Vanzetti.) Communists were not deeply involved in the struggle against the Ku Klux Klan in the
twenties, or in behalf of sharecroppers in the thirties, or in
resistance to Paul McNutt's military law in Indiana or
Frank Hague's personal law in Hudson County, New Jersey. Where communists were involved in those earlier
years, it was usually in activities in themselves legal or even
praiseworthy. Often they were defending the rights of Ne-
groes and workers.

Nevertheless, from 1919 on, plenty was happening inside and outside of the Socialist Party to make me reluc-

tantly aware that Lenin's communism was the enemy not only of individual freedom but of ordinary fair play whenever its leaders thought that freedom and fair play stood in their way.

Like the vast majority of my countrymen, I had greatly rejoiced in the downfall of the czar of Russia. Lenin's later triumph raised in my mind some doubts, but I thought his enemies were worse than he, and that the revolutionary emergency extenuated, if it did not justify, his denials of freedom. I remember that, back in 1919, I held a meeting in my house, no hall being available, for Nuorteva and Maartens, unofficial Bolshevik delegates to the United States. Before that, Postmaster General Burleson had barred my magazine, *The World Tomorrow*, from the mails and had threatened me with jail for life, or something like it, because in the magazine I had written an article sharply questioning American intervention at Archangel and Vladivostok. (This, incidentally, was the only case known to me in which President Wilson directly interfered to call off his prosecutors—but that's another story.)

Things like this, however, bought me no immunity from communist attacks after World War I was over. Almost immediately the self-proclaimed Bolsheviks set out to capture or break the Socialist Party. Their tactics and their open contempt for democracy in the struggles which split the Socialist Party greatly disturbed me. The public climax of communist intolerance was reached when communists invaded a great mass meeting at Madison Square

Garden, called to protest Dollfuss' attack on the socialist workers in Vienna in 1934. The organized invaders, armed with various weapons, broke up a serious and impressive meeting. I was away at the time and on my return was shocked at the equivocal attitude of the American Civil Liberties Union, some of whose leaders were at that time so emotionally committed to the defense of communists that they made no proper and effective protest. They finally, under pressure, uttered some mild condemnation. Then and there, I resolved to campaign for a single standard of belief in civil liberties in the USSR as in the USA as a condition of membership on the governing board of the ACLU. It was slow business. Not until 1940 did the Board adopt the resolution which established that policy.

Nevertheless, I cannot say that my own attitude toward communism, or my understanding of it, was always clear, precise, and wholly consistent. On general principles, I believed in joint action on specific issues, without too lofty a standard of purity in selecting one's allies—for instance, in the struggle against fascism. I was considerably impressed by the proclaimed desire of communists for a united front against fascism after Stalin made that his policy for American as well as European communists early in 1935. Fascism seemed to me the enemy above all others, and communists fought fascism. I had great hope that in Russia terror and oppression were subsiding. I learned belatedly of the horrors of the man-made famine in the Ukraine in 1934. Here in America, I hoped—and worked—that socialists

rather than communists might win control of some of the
various organizations now listed by the Attorney General
as subversive. (This was especially true of the North American Committee to Aid Spanish Democracy.)

There was a strong element in the Socialist Party that
feared that I, and more especially some of my younger
friends, were too willing to work with communists. The
rather confused struggles concerning the correct socialist
attitude toward communism, along with certain other factors, led to a considerable secession from the Party in 1936.
By one of history's ironies, those who left us found themselves soon thereafter working side by side with communists in the newly organized American Labor Party in New
York State for the re-election of Franklin Delano Roosevelt, while the Socialist Party went its way untainted—save
for a brief, unhappy flirtation with Trotskyists—by contact
with communists.

What opened my eyes—and the eyes of most American
socialists—to the nature of communism as the irredeemable
foe of justice and liberty to individuals were the purge
trials of 1936–1938 and the communist intrigues for power
in loyalist Spain during the Civil War, in which, at a great
price to the Spaniards, they gave some aid to the Loyalists.
A visit to Russia and Spain in 1937 completed my education. Yet even so I was surprised by the enormity of the
Hitler-Stalin Pact in 1939.

Even the memory of this educational process is pain-
ful. But I realize in retrospect that I should be thankful for

my many advantages in learning the truth. As early as my return from Europe in 1937, I felt morally obligated to write about communism and liberty. In 1938 together with Joel Seidman, now a professor in the University of Chicago, I wrote a pamphlet, *Russia: Democracy or Dictatorship*, which was finally published by the League for Industrial Democracy in 1939. (That organization had tried for months to get a factual communist answer to publish in the same pamphlet—all in vain.)

Reading that pamphlet today, I am inclined to apologize for our ignorance or our timidity in stating the brutal facts. But ours was about the first well-documented, factual description of communism's increasing denials of freedom published in America. The great Russian contribution to victory over Hitler, a contribution made only after Hitler attacked Russia, never seemed to me a reason for changing my painfully formed judgment of Stalinism. Therefore, during World War II, and for about a year thereafter, I was often reproached not only by Rooseveltians but by Republicans for my lack of faith in Stalin's good intentions.[*]

Since I am not writing either an autobiography or a history of the radical movement in America, I content myself with this outline of my relations both to the organized defense of civil liberty and to the communist movement.

---

[*] See for example the Town Meeting of the Air on "Russia and America—Post-war Rivals or Allies?" (published in *America's Town Meeting of the Air Bulletin*, May 31, 1945) and observe Raymond Moley's optimism in arguing against me.

Some of my experiences may require further discussion later in other connections. I refer to them in beginning this book so that the reader can judge for himself my background and qualifications for discussing American policy concerning the rights of communists and devotees of other totalitarian movements. Certainly my record in these tumultuous years justifies no boasts of omniscience or infallibility. I like to believe that it is a record of honest search after truth.

My experiences have, I think, given me some understanding of the diverse psychological reactions of disillusioned communists and liberals who once held rather higher opinions than mine of the nature of communism. Some of them reacted violently. They swung to Roman Catholic or other authoritarianism; often, like the founders and editors of the *Freeman,* they became more orthodox in economics than the United States Chamber of Commerce. Others, however, although sorrowfully convinced in their minds of the true nature of communism, do not easily shake off their old emotional attitudes, formed in the days when for them to defend communists was, they thought, to defend liberty and to crusade against fascism. Their instinctive reaction is a livelier suspicion and dislike of anticommunists than of communists. They may have been finally and reluctantly persuaded of Alger Hiss's guilt, but they cannot forgive Whittaker Chambers. It is an understandable emotion, but not helpful in forming policy in the field of civil liberty.

II.

The Jeffersonian Ideal in Practice

SINCE THE LIBERTIES which we are discussing are apparently well protected by the Bill of Rights of the federal Constitution, it has in our day become the fashion—rather too much the fashion—for those who are concerned in protecting our fundamental freedoms to discuss them mainly in terms of legalistic reference to that historic document. Oratorically, our freedoms are usually acclaimed and defended by eloquent quotations from writers like Milton, Locke, John Stuart Mill; statesmen like Jefferson and Lincoln; and jurists like Justices Holmes, Brandeis, and Hand.

Eulogists of the Bill of Rights often overlook the fact that some of the hardest-won rights of the individual against the state were inserted in the Constitution itself. Thus, that document, as it came from the Constitutional

24

Convention, narrowly defines treason and the proof of it; forbids bills of attainder and ex post facto laws; provides that the trials for all federal crimes, except cases of impeachment, shall be by jury in the state in which the crime was committed; and—most important of all—stipulates that "the privilege of the writ of habeas corpus shall not be suspended, unless when in cases of rebellion or invasion the public safety may require it."

To obtain the adoption of the Constitution by men who believed that they had fought a successful revolutionary war for the sake of freedom, it was agreed that the rights mentioned in the Constitution should be expressly supplemented in a Bill of Rights to be embodied in amendments to the Constitution. This agreement was promptly carried out under the new government without any substantial opposition. The Fourth and Eighth Amendments spelled out constitutional protection of the individual against "unreasonable searches and seizures," excessive bail requirements, excessive fines, and cruel and unusual punishments. The Fifth, Sixth, and Seventh gave the citizens guarantees of due process of law in civil and criminal procedures. The First Amendment, the most vital to our discussion, forbade Congress to pass any law impairing freedom of conscience by the establishment of any religion, or the denial of freedom of speech, press, and petition. In short, the Bill of Rights established freedom of worship and speech, two of the four freedoms later made famous by

Franklin Delano Roosevelt, and, at least in terms of formal respect, gave those freedoms an almost sacrosanct quality.

This formal acceptance of the Bill of Rights by our fathers and by ourselves has caused us too often to rest our case for freedom upon the authority of a sacred document, forgetting that our liberties were won by a long historic struggle and are in constant need of vigilance if they are to be maintained. It has never been easy for mankind in daily practice to give moral weight and legal recognition to the duty of a government, a ruling class, or the community itself to be just to those to whom it does not wish to be just and to tolerate the noncomformer or the dissenter.

Moreover, it is usually forgotten that it was not until the adoption of the Fourteenth Amendment that the guarantees of the federal Bill of Rights were extended to the protection of individuals under state laws; and it was not until the Gitlow case in 1920 that the Supreme Court began to apply the federal doctrine within the states. It is an interesting historical fact that the great extension of the doctrine of civil liberties by Supreme Court decision came almost simultaneously with the emergence of new problems for Jeffersonian democrats because of the rise of totalitarianism, communist and fascist.

Behind the Jeffersonian ideal lay a long history of events often dramatic, often tragic. For the freedom to follow his conscience, Socrates had drunk the hemlock. To bear witness to their faith, prophets, saints, and martyrs in the great Judeo-Christian tradition had unflinchingly faced prison and death rather than deny a God whose love gave to each of His children dignity and worth. To give political reality to individual rights, generations of Englishmen had struggled to win victories which began when the barons wrested Magna Carta from King John.

The American colonists had carried on that selfsame struggle in their new home. They had come, many of them, to the distant wilderness for the sake of freedom to worship God as they pleased. To be sure, this passion for their own freedom by no means taught the colonists tolerance. The liberty for which "true believers" have always contended is liberty to establish the truth which, once in power, they stand ready to enforce against dissent for the protection of the individual and society. The Judeo-Christian tradition, with its respect for the individual, played a great role in laying the basis for freedom, but it did not by any means automatically guarantee it. Not only Roman Catholicism but Calvinism and most other forms of Protestantism were highly authoritarian. To this day, the authoritarian aspect of religion is one of the elements which often contributes to popular intolerance of dissent. It must be remembered that John Milton's magnificent defense of freedom of publication did not apply to the civil rights of atheists or Jews or Catholics. At least as late as 1825, some American states restricted the rights of Jews and atheists to hold office. A century later there was still a law on the statute books of

New Jersey which would bar the testimony of an atheist in court, a legal position not formally upset until challenged in a case argued by the contemporary champion of civil liberties Morris Ernst.

Nevertheless, despite the intolerance of the early Puritans, the spirit of bigotry died faster in the new world than in the old. The very conditions of life on the great frontier made for respect for the individual and for his freedom. Indeed, that provocative writer Walter Prescott Webb attributes the rise of modern democracy in which free individuals are all-important almost solely to the frontier and the conditions of life on it.* Like many another man who gets hold of a good idea, Mr. Webb presses his theory too far as the sole explanation of our freedoms. But unquestionably the existence of what he calls the "Great Frontier" had immense influence in developing the kind of men for whom and to whom Jefferson spoke, and the end of that frontier tends of itself to raise problems in the interpretation and preservation of individual freedom.

Historically, not even under the lusty influence of a great frontier, not even with the sanctions of the Bill of Rights, did freedom go unchallenged in the new federal republic. John Adams, second president of the United States, had to guide a young nation, insecure in its unity, torn by the passions which the French Revolution and the Napoleonic Wars had stirred. Not without provocation, his Federalist Party put through Congress the famous, or in-

* *The Great Frontier* (Houghton Mifflin, 1952).

famous, Alien and Sedition Acts. These laws flouted not only the spirit but the letter of the Bill of Rights which had been adopted so easily a few years earlier. The principal Alien law permitted the federal government summarily to deport aliens; and another lengthened to fourteen years the time an alien must spend in America before he could be naturalized. To his credit be it said, John Adams never urged this legislation and never used the law to deport an alien.

The Sedition Act, however, was a different and more serious matter. Under it, the federal government made twenty-four arrests, including the editors of the four leading Democratic papers. There were ten convictions, one of the latter solely because a man circulated a petition— this although the Bill of Rights expressly guaranteed the right to petition. Perhaps the most outrageous case was that of an obscure citizen, David Brown of Dedham, Massachusetts. He had put up a liberty pole carrying the following inscription: "No Stamp Act, No Sedition, No Alien Bills, No Land Tax; Downfall to the Tyrants of America, peace and retirement to the President, long live the Vice-President [Thomas Jefferson] and the Minority; may moral virtue be the basis of civil government." For this, he was convicted, sentenced to serve eighteen months' imprisonment and to pay a fine of four hundred dollars. He could not pay the fine and therefore had to remain in jail, where he stayed for two years, until pardoned by Jefferson on his assumption of office.

It follows from this historical statement that the great triumph for civil liberties in the United States of America was less the adoption of the Bill of Rights than Jefferson's electoral victory, resulting in the "revolution" of 1801.

That revolution justified Hamilton's confidence in the essential moderation of one of his great political opponents, Thomas Jefferson, as compared with the other, Aaron Burr. When the House of Representatives was preparing to vote in order to break the electoral tie between Jefferson and Burr, there were Federalists who were with difficulty persuaded from throwing their support to Burr and thus elevating him to the presidency.

In Washington, President Jefferson built the strength of the new nation. His states-rights leanings and his strict constitutionalism did not deter him from an act of high statesmanship, the purchase of the Louisiana Territory. His doctrine of civil liberties did not prevent him from pressing —some historians have said overpressing—the trial of Aaron Burr for treason, or from supporting that curious character General Wilkinson as virtual dictator in New Orleans. Burr's acts did not fall within the tolerance of the man who in the confused days of the Confederation had condoned Daniel Shays's rebellion against real wrongs with the remark that the tree of liberty would flourish the better if it were watered every twenty years with blood.

The revulsion against the Alien and Sedition Acts and the general atmosphere of the frontier formed for generations a strong protection for civil liberties. There were exceptions. It took something of a struggle within the states to win universal male suffrage—and, much later, votes for women. It took a harder and longer struggle to establish rights for labor. Occasional ill will against immigrants flared up; the Supreme Order of the Star-Spangled Banner, part of what was commonly called the Know-Nothings, a secret political party inspired by dislike of Irish Catholics, gained considerable strength in the years between 1850 and 1854. Its life was short. Freedom of speech and the press helped to keep these struggles free from great violence. There was little need for intervention by federal courts.

The one terrible blot upon freedom in the growing nation was Negro slavery. The supreme struggle for liberty was directed to the prevention of any extension of slavery and to its ultimate extinction. In this struggle, both federal and state governments were involved. But chattel slaves were property, and to them neither the federal nor the corresponding state guarantees of constitutional rights applied. Fugitive-slave laws were not fought on the basis of any appeal to legal doctrines of civil liberties. The Dred Scott decision of the Supreme Court that the residence of a Negro slave in a free state did not make him a free man was a factor in bringing upon our country the tragedy of the Civil War, but that decision did not directly involve the Bill of Rights.

There were cases involving academic liberty and freedom of speech and the press which grew out of the struggle against slavery. There were cases of mob violence, of which the most shameful in the North was the "martyrdom"—the word is John Quincy Adams'—of Elijah Lovejoy in Alton, Illinois, solely for asserting his moral and constitutional right to oppose slavery.

None other than Andrew Jackson, today hailed along with Jefferson as a patron saint of the Democratic Party, urged Congress, unsuccessfully, to prohibit under severe penalties the circulation in the Southern states, through the mail, of "incendiary" publications, intended, he said, to "incite the slaves to insurrection." Various Southern states forbade the circulation of antislavery literature.

All this was a sorry departure from the Jeffersonian ideal, and to protect that ideal there was little or no appeal to the federal courts. Federal law was rarely involved. Nevertheless, public opinion was profoundly affected by the existence of the Declaration of Independence and the Bill of Rights. Perhaps one should marvel that in pioneer communities, often prone to direct action, an issue so fraught with emotion as slavery was for many years before the Civil War, so freely discussed without frequent police intervention or mob violence.

The Civil War brought with it many restraints on an untrammeled freedom of speech and the press under the federal government. Within most of the Northern states, to say nothing of the border states, there were vocal sympathizers with the South, men and women of very doubtful loyalty to the Union. I remember my surprise and disappointment when I first learned that under the government of my great hero, Abraham Lincoln, there was an estimated total of 38,000 arrests of men and women who were brought before military commissions, most of them on charges that did not involve overt acts of violence or disloyalty, but merely expressions of opinion in speech or the press. However, in the experience of two world wars, I came to understand how great was the provocation in a civil war for the action which Lincoln took. He himself defended it in his famous question: "Are all laws but one to go unexecuted? And the government itself to go to pieces, lest that one be violated?" In the same statement he went on to argue that under the Constitution, he had full power to suspend the writ of habeas corpus "when in cases of rebellion or invasion, the public safety may require." Lincoln occasionally interfered to curb his subordinates and at one point (February, 1862) granted an extensive amnesty. But a few months later, he ordered a general suspension of the writ of habeas corpus which previously he had suspended only in certain areas. Such efforts as the courts made to interfere were unsuccessful. Imprisonment was usually brief.

Soon after the end of the war, the Supreme Court handed down a decision, *Ex parte* Milligan, which became a classic expression in defense of civil rights even in time of war. Lambden P. Milligan was arrested and taken before a military commission in October, 1864. His appeal was slow in reaching the Supreme Court and was not decided until

1866. The Court then declared that the president had no
legal power under the Constitution to suspend the writ of
habeas corpus or institute martial law, except in areas
where the civil courts were unable to function. The important declaration was this: "So long as the courts were
functioning, martial law cannot arise from a threatened
invasion." In World War I, the federal government found
ways to deal on the whole as drastically with freedom of
speech and press as in the Civil War, although there was
no rebellion or any threat of serious invasion of the United
States. In the process it utilized the machinery of the established courts.

　　The Civil War was followed by the adoption of the
Thirteenth, Fourteenth, and Fifteenth Amendments, abol-
ishing slavery, prohibiting the denial of citizenship rights,
and guaranteeing—on paper—equal rights of suffrage to
citizens of the United States, white or colored. The Fourteenth Amendment expressly declared: "No State shall
make or enforce any law which shall abridge the privileges
or immunities of citizens of the United States; nor shall any
State deprive any person of life, liberty, or property, without due process of law; nor deny to any person within its
jurisdiction the equal protection of the laws." It is a plain
and sorry fact that for half a century, this amendment was
virtually ignored except in the protection that it gave under
a succession of conservative justices to corporations threatened by adverse state legislation.

　　Congress passed certain laws to protect individual

rights in Reconstruction days, but they rapidly became dead letters. It was not until 1920, in the Gitlow case, that the Supreme Court acted formally to guarantee due process and respect for the First Amendment by state courts. It accepted the appeal of Benjamin Gitlow, convicted of violating the so-called anti-anarchy law of New York State. The Court held that Mr. Gitlow, one of the founders of the Communist Party, was entitled to be heard on the question of the violation of the First Amendment. It then ruled that the New York law, as applied in the Gitlow case, did not violate the constitutional guarantees.*

Following the Gitlow case, the Supreme Court rendered many decisions in defense of individual rights against restrictive laws and judicial practices within the states. In general, between the two world wars, its decisions tended substantially to protect individual freedom and notably to advance equality of civil rights.

Its record on cases arising in the first world war, under war conditions, had been a very different matter. President Woodrow Wilson, the Congress, and the courts of his wartime administration had no such excuse for a frightened intolerance as existed in Abraham Lincoln's troubled years. There was criticism of the war and outspoken political opposition to it, which mostly took the form of open political agitation for a negotiated peace, but there was virtually no sabotage and no organized opposition to the draft after

---

* Mr. Gitlow served his sentence and became a high official in the Communist Party, which he left about 1929, becoming a severe critic of it.

the small and wholly unsuccessful "green-corn rebellion" in Oklahoma in the very early days of the war. Yet under legislation passed by Congress, men and women were arrested and convicted for frivolous reasons. I vividly remember an occasion when I visited President Harding in behalf of the war prisoners (I was born in his home town, Marion, Ohio, and once had carried his paper, *The Star*, on a delivery route). The President rather dramatically pointed to a pile of papers on his desk and said to me, "These applications for pardon cause me the greatest concern. Do you remember old —— in Marion?" I said that I did. He was a well-known and well-loved German-American who talked with an almost comic accent. "Well," said the President, "from these papers, I gather that the man I pardoned was just like him: He was old and somewhat of a burden upon his family; he was convicted for some remarks that one of his relatives alleged that he made, remarks which certainly did not endanger the government of the United States."

It was in connection with the Schenck case in World War I that Justice Oliver Wendell Holmes, with the concurrence of a unanimous court, laid down the now famous doctrine of "clear and present danger." This doctrine will be discussed later in its more recent application. It is generally admitted that it has a certain logical force. As the famous jurist pointed out, it does make a difference when and where one cries fire. Later on he and Justice Brandeis were to challenge the judgment of their colleagues in certain applications of this doctrine. At the time of the court's decision, I doubted if Schenck's action in mailing comparatively few draft leaflets to potential draftees (soon after the passage of the draft act) created "clear and present danger." There was no evidence that it obstructed the draft. What was far worse was Justice Holmes's concurrence in the extension of his principle in the appeal of Eugene V. Debs against his conviction for constructive obstruction of recruiting and enlistment. This, I thought and still think, was an abuse of the First Amendment. Debs had made a public address against the war to the convention of a political party (the Socialists in Ohio). He asked no one to refuse the draft. Clear and present danger existed only in alarmed imaginations. Nevertheless, one must admit that there may be "clear and present danger" in an emergency, however possible is error in judging its existence.

What happened to civil liberty in the United States during World War I and immediately thereafter—for example in the expulsion of the Socialist assemblymen in New York and the enactment of the repressive Lusk laws— led a great many of us to believe that our democracy could not engage in a major war without an abridgment of personal liberty, approximating that under a totalitarian regime. None other than Charles Evans Hughes told the alumni of Harvard Law School in 1920 that "we may well wonder in view of the precedents now established whether constitutional government as heretofore maintained in this republic could survive another great war even victoriously waged."

In World War II, our fears were happily refuted. For most Americans, freedom of speech and discussion were well protected. The Supreme Court itself in one or two instances decided in favor of appellants, convicted in lower courts of seditious utterances, whose cases had not appealed enough to the majority of the directors of the ACLU to warrant their support. The most notorious case, brought under political pressure from liberals, was the trial in Washington, D.C. of twenty-eight strangely assorted persons for seditious conspiracy. It became farcical; the harassed judge died during the proceedings; the government eventually dropped the case.

The principal—sometimes I have been tempted to think the only—reason for this great degree of freedom of speech was the fact that World War II was unique in American experience. It was our only war to which there was not a considerable political opposition. The Japanese attack on Pearl Harbor without declaration of war completely silenced the rather formidable political opposition to American military intervention in the war. The communists, who had denounced the European war as imperialistic, had changed their policy overnight when Hitler attacked Russia. For the duration of the war they were enthusiastic American patriots. (On several occasions they made feeble and unsuccessful gestures to get either the government or a mob to prevent my speaking, especially during the campaign of 1944. I was allegedly unpatriotic because of my criticism of Roosevelt's formula of unconditional surrender and my skepticism concerning Roosevelt's approach to peace by what looked like appeasement of Stalin.) Whatever sympathy Hitler may have kept among German-Americans, they organized no opposition whatever to the war and they practiced no sabotage. The only important cases, few in number, involved German spies and saboteurs sent into the country.

Nevertheless, despite the good record of respect for most men's civil liberties in World War II, that conflict saw the establishment of a precedent which in practice threatens the protections of the Bill of Rights in any wartime situation in which the executive and the military may decide that there is a grave emergency. Today no responsible student acquainted with the facts will argue that there was any excuse of necessity, much less moral justification, for the wholesale evacuation of Japanese and Japanese-Americans from the West Coast without trial or hearing. (It is interesting to note that in the Hawaiian Islands, under direct attack, and where over one-third of the population was either Japanese or Japanese-American, no such action was thought necessary; nor was there any trouble as a result.) Yet the majority of the Supreme Court held that the government had legal power for its action on the West Coast. No act of any American court in any war so completely nullified effective protection of civil liberty.

Clearly, on this historical record, the protection of civil liberties in wartime by the Bill of Rights has been inconsiderable. Popular feeling protected much critical speech in the War of 1812, the Mexican War, and the Spanish-American War. The existence of the nation wasn't felt to be in jeopardy and there were powerful groups opposed to the wars. The situation was very different in the great wars. During most of our national history our people have felt no conflict between liberty and security. When they have experienced that conflict, often without anything like adequate reason, popular opinion has generally supported or outstripped the government in enforcing conformity to the patriotic ideal in words as well as deeds.

The same devotion to security supports the denial of civil liberty, including the denial or severe limitation of conscience, inherent in compulsory military service. Conscription for males, in itself the supreme expression of state power over the individual's life and conscience, has been accepted in war and in preparation for—or allegedly the prevention of—war. Gone are the days when an orator or statesman will attack conscription as Daniel Webster successfully attacked it in the War of 1812. The inequities of the Civil War draft were avoided or greatly abated by the Selective Service drafts of two world wars. The laws gave some limited and partial exception to conscientious objectors, but they required a religious, usually a creedal, basis for legalized objection. Selective Service, to which all are theoretically subject, is supported in great emergency not only by an overriding devotion to security but by a feeling that somehow such service is an approach to a democratic equality of sacrifice. It is an approach which in the nature of things never reaches that goal.*

In spite of this, if I had been writing this book, let us say, in the year 1946, I should have been reasonably optimistic about the state of civil liberties in America. We were repenting the evacuation of the Japanese. There was no equivalent to the rise and growth of the Ku Klux Klan in the early twenties. That ugly organization had subsided almost as fast as it had arisen. Fortunately, its rise had coincided with a period of prosperity. I still tremble when I think what might have happened if the organization had not been so thoroughly discredited by its own mistakes and the latent good sense of the American people before the depression era of the 1930's. Following the decline of the Klan, the years saw the birth and death of a large number of native fascist organizations, mostly regional. No leader or slogan united them successfully in a nationwide drive against civil liberties.

Our apparent success in preserving civil liberties during World War II was not followed at the war's end by any rapid revival of these ugly and ignorant semifascist organizations. Neither was there after World War II any such campaign to break labor unions as followed World War I.

---

* On conscientious objection in World War I, see my book *Is Conscience a Crime?* (Vanguard Press); for World War II, see *Conscription of Conscience* by Mulford Sibley and Philip Jacob (Cornell Studies in Civil Liberty, Cornell University Press, 1952).

The legislation of the Roosevelt Era and the rapid growth of unions in strength had virtually ended the near-war waged by powerful corporations against labor's right to organize—the nature of which was documented by the report of the LaFollette Committee on Civil Liberties as late as 1937.

This brief historical review up to 1946 shows that pragmatic Americans, profoundly influenced by the Jeffersonian idea, nevertheless gave it far less than absolute and consistent support. They had generally given assent to John Stuart Mill's dictum that "over his own mind and body, the individual is sovereign." But from the beginning of their national history, they had given less than full faith and credit to that principle by inserting, in law until the Civil War and in practice thereafter, the adjective *white* before the noun "individual."

These same Americans had usually agreed with the proposition that truth could best win its own victory over error in the market place of ideas without intervention by the state's police. In practice, this opinion was not always carried out. As a matter of fact, history gives dubious support to the notion that truth always wins; it gives far more support to a disbelief in the competence of governments or mobs to determine truth. Heresy is by no means always right—false prophets have probably outnumbered the true —but heresy has been the growing point of society; society uses force to check dissent at its peril. Every great religion and the whole body of science began with a challenge to accepted traditions.

An absolute philosophy of freedom, permitting no exception, is difficult—even impossible—to state. Perhaps the best-known and most useful formula is Mill's famous declaration that "the sole end for which mankind are warranted, individually or collectively, in interfering with the liberty of action of any of their numbers is self-protection." The state can act only "to prevent harm to others. . . . a man's own good either physical or moral is not a sufficient warrant."

Helpful as this statement has been in justifying our civil liberties, it cannot be said to lay down an infallible rule of easy application. What harms others? "The preaching of a heresy that jeopardizes men's immortal souls." Thus bigoted Torquemada might have answered. "The agitator whose words impel the simple soldier to desert," the humane Lincoln once decided. "The unbridled pursuit of personal profit," the socialist and labor organizer would say, while in our own day, the advocate of free enterprise stridently insists that powerful labor unions and the intervention of the state in the economic order jeopardize the only economic system in which individual freedom can flourish.

Practically, in our own history of dealing with the Mormon Church, we Americans have held that freedom of religion or conscience does not justify a practice of polygamy which society has come to regard as socially harmful. Neither, in time of epidemic, have American government agencies refrained from compulsory vaccination or from enforcing other rules of health and hygiene even upon those who say that they reject them for conscientious reasons. In support of this sort of compulsion, we have a solid body of evidence that the individual loses little and society gains greatly by preventing disastrous epidemics.

Clearly there is no simple principle which permits us easily to identify individual freedom with social well-being. Even in a well-ordered and democratic society there are emergencies in which balance must be consciously sought. But in the century and a half since the Jeffersonian revolution, his working principle that the state may interfere only to punish an overt act (modified in our day by granting the power of the state to interfere to prevent an immediately impending overt act) has triumphantly met the pragmatic test—it has worked.

Occasionally that principle has been phrased by libertarians in terms which might suggest that an agitator is always morally praiseworthy so long as he is unsuccessful in provoking sabotage or violence. It is not for that reason that during most of our history discussion of possible future violence has wisely been allowed to go unpunished, but rather because the attempt to punish a man for speech, unaccompanied by overt acts of violence cannot in the light of the historical record be carried out without dangerously jeopardizing all freedom to challenge outworn customs and ancient wrongs. Truth has won enough victories to keep our nation secure.

Let Americans fearful that individual liberty is inconsistent with national security take a fresh look at our history. Until 1924 the United States was receiving peacefully tens, then hundreds, of thousands of immigrants from every country in Europe every year. They brought their own customs and languages. In an atmosphere of freedom they formed with the descendants of older immigrants a united nation. There was indeed some occasional popular intolerance, but no legal discrimination. This peaceful growth of one America, one nation out of many peoples, has no parallel in the history of mankind.

It was precisely in this atmosphere of freedom that unity grew, and that America escaped the difficulties which so often have plagued multilanguaged nations in Europe. When two world wars put this unity to the supreme test, from cities like Milwaukee and Buffalo the sons of Germans and Poles marched off together to the conflict and there were no riots at home.

We are proud still to call ours a young nation. Hence we forget what we should remember: Our nation under the present Constitution has had a longer life unchallenged and unchanged by violent rebellion than any great nation on earth except Great Britain. And Britain has been in a very real sense the mother of civil liberty. Our Civil War was not a revolt against the Constitution or the general Jeffersonian theory. It arose, rather, from the attempt to preserve

and extend the infamy of chattel slavery. Not our devotion to liberty but our denial of it to a race of slaves challenged our national security—a fact to be written on men's
hearts in these troublous times.

III.

Communism, the Foe of Freedom

AS THE NEW YEAR DAWNED in 1947, an observer could have made a powerful argument that civil liberties stood at their highest point in American history. There were laws on the statute books of the federal government and the various states which might lend themselves to repression, but they slept. There had been evil exceptions, but on the whole, the cause of civil rights for all regardless of race was progressing. Free speech had been strengthened by recent court decisions.

Of course, there were social pressures adverse to true freedom. These, strange as it may now seem, came largely from communists and so-called liberals. Pro-Russian, if not pro-communist, feeling was powerful not only in Hollywood but in various civic forums, so that, for instance, speakers—myself one of them—were rather frequently banned from discussing communism on the platform because we were allegedly "redbaiters." As late as the fall of 1946, a man named Joseph McCarthy, Wisconsin war veteran and youthful judge, thought it both safe and advisable to accept without protest or even explanation communist and pro-communist support in the "open" Republican primary in order to defeat Robert LaFollette, Jr., for the senatorial nomination.

It was Stalin's aggressive imperialism which ended the honeymoon. The Czechoslovak coup was the decisive turning point in American sentiment. As our people increasingly resented imperialistic communism in foreign affairs, they became better aware of its universal significance as the total enemy of the dignity of man and his right to freedom of mind and conscience. Unfortunately, in learning the necessity of fighting communism in the name of liberty, our people did not learn how to fight it without in some degree imitating its oppressive tactics. McCarthyism is really the ally of the foe it purports to fight.

But before we discuss McCarthyism we must briefly examine communism and the nature of the extraordinary peril which it presents.

Communism is a secular religion which seeks universal power over the bodies, minds, and souls of men. Upon this secular religion, international in scope and appeal, Lenin and Stalin, as heads of the great Soviet state, imposed a Russian imperial control against which thus far only Tito has successfully revolted. This secular religion, its hierarchy now horribly corrupted by power, seeks the ultimate earthly salvation and happiness of mankind through the achievement of its own type of economic collectivism. The Messiah is nominally the working class and the apocalypse a communist revolution. Mankind is an abstraction. Individual men are completely expendable in the service of the cause or those who exploit it. In reality, the Messiah is not the working class but the Communist Party. And when the Party gains power the Messiah becomes a despot; but since the Party as a whole cannot function as an absolute totalitarian ruler, an inner circle takes over, and in that circle one man eventually becomes the quasi-divine leader. (In this role Stalin, after struggle, succeeded Lenin. As I write, there is a kind of government by a group which minimizes the cult of the leader. I suspect that such government is temporary and masks a struggle for power, in which already Beria, for a short time a leading contender, has been wiped out by Malenkov and his present allies.)

Within the Party and for its supporters, there is but one great commandment, laid down by Lenin himself: Thou shalt believe what the Party tells you and do whatsoever is necessary in the judgment of the Party to advance its interests. Every change of line, every lie or deceit or act of violence thus commanded, is right and holy.

Thirty-five years after the Bolshevik revolution, Stalin, on the eve of his death, had liquidated in his great purges all who had been his comrades in the executive committee

of the Party at the time of the revolution—except those
who had died natural deaths—and hundreds of thousands
of others. He ruled over an empire in which veritable chattel slavery, this time to an omnipotent police state, had
been re-established in horrible work camps to which men
could be sent by proceedings having no trace of fair and
orderly process. The only question at issue is the number
of these slaves; during a debate with Peter Viereck, Corliss
Lamont, a champion of the Bolshevik regime with some
minor criticisms, put the number at *only* two million; other,
and I think more expert, authorities put the number at
ten, twelve, or even twenty million. Such amnesty and
other concessions as the new regime has granted have not
essentially changed this evil system.

"Free" labor is not too much better off than the prisoners in respect to freedom. The variations in pay are, per-
centagewise, greater than in the capitalist USA. Internal
passports and work cards are required of workers. There
are trade unions, but there is no right to strike and the
trade unions are company unions in relation to the police
state.

Modern techniques of communication and modern
methods of psychology have made the Kremlin's control
over thought, communication, and all creative and intellectual work more effectively absolute than ever before in
human history. Stalin was the final authority in philosophy,
the arts, and the sciences, notably biology. He not only
shaped present history but rewrote the past in accordance

with his judgment of political necessity. His successors will not easily or voluntarily renounce similar authority.

It used to be said that the features of communism which were most objectionable to believers in the rights of men were Asiatic or at least Russian in origin and would not appear in Western communism. The plain truth is that whatever their origin these denials of human dignity and right are woven into the warp and woof of Leninist communism. If it were not so grim in its implication, it would be amusing to recall the pains with which American communists ever since the first world war have imitated the manners and morals of their Russian masters in dealing not only with the general public but with socialists and labor unionists.

Let one comparatively unimportant episode illustrate my point: Back in Herbert Hoover's time, I had occasion in behalf of the Socialist Party to testify in an inquiry concerning a military program for America. Testifying ahead of me, Fiorello H. LaGuardia, then a congressman, proposed a constitutional amendment designed to make easier the task of total mobilization for war. I criticized the amendment as fascist, rather than socialist, in its probable effect if immediately adopted, although I said that in the event of war, "I should be for it"—the amendment. Everyone at the hearing, including communist representatives, knew exactly what I meant. But weeks later all over the United States, in their press and on their platforms, the communists denounced me, citing an official government record as their authority, for saying that "in the event of war, I should be for it"—that is, war. Lenin has had apt pupils all over the world for his doctrine that any lie or deceit is justified in furthering the cause.

The most conspicuous proof that the knock on the door at two in the morning, the star-chamber proceedings, the concentration camps, the extorted confessions, are not peculiarly Russian is to be seen in the imitation of these practices not only by the communists of China, which is an Asian country, but in the satellite states in Europe. Czechoslovakia is the most Western of the satellites in habit of mind and in experience with democracy, yet it was precisely in Czechoslovakia, in the purge of the once powerful communist leader Rudolph Slansky and his associates, that the communist technique was most clearly revealed in all its horror. There is, alas, nothing new in extorted confessions. What is new in the communist procedure is the complete destruction of the individual and his integrity by forcing from him confessions of acts which he not only did not commit, but which were completely out of line with his own record and character. Slansky was a cruel man who might well have confessed anti-Zionist activity. He was instead forced to confess to Zionist plots. And this happened in Prague, where that great democrat and philosophical liberal Thomas Masaryk had once been a father to his people.

In Lenin's time every communist party in every country was constrained to absolute obedience to the general communist line, but while Lenin lived there was a certain rudimentary democracy within the communist parties of the world and in the Comintern itself. It remained for Stalin to make the whole communist movement the obedient servant of the Kremlin, a fifth column for Russian aggrandizement. The American movement, as will be shown, is no exception. It is part of a movement, international in scope, seeking universal power, controlled by the heads of a foreign government engaged in cold war with the United States. Like every branch of Leninist communism, it is by its nature conspiratorial. Its own scriptures and its conduct in power show it to be in complete opposition to the Jeffersonian theory and practice of civil liberties. In days gone by, certain American communists, less cautious than now, assured me that while they were a minority they would demand all the rights that they could get under the American theory, and that believers of the Jeffersonian type of democracy should extend those rights to them. "But," said they, "of course, in power, we could not and would not grant them to our critics and our enemies. The ultimate freedom of the workers requires a vigorous suppression of bourgeois opposition and criticism."

It has been years since any defender of communism has effectively denied these charges of horrible tyranny over the bodies, minds, and souls of men. There has scarcely been an effort at denial. Nevertheless, there is a stubborn reluctance in some liberal circles to admit the logical implications of communist totalitarianism and the gravity of the problems it presents to supporters of the Jeffersonian ideal. Various excuses or pleas in extenuation are frequently offered.

One meets contentions such as these: There must be something good in communism or it couldn't have been so amazingly successful. Why, if communism is so evil, is it so widely supported, not only behind the iron curtain but throughout the world? Above all, why have Americans, brought up in a tradition of liberty, become communists? Why do many of them remain communists? What real harm have they done us?

The sources of communist strength are many and difficult to summarize. It should be remembered that Leninism is not the first movement whose dynamic power among men has been great despite its denial of liberty. Jules Monnerot in his *Psychology and Sociology of Communism,* the ablest book on the subject which has been published, calls communism the twentieth-century Islam and examines in detail the various sources of its strength as a secular religion concerned for "truth"—its peculiar truth—rather than freedom. The Polish poet Czeslaw Milosz, today a refugee from communism, in his brilliant book *The Captive Mind* describes in terms of his own experience and observation the curious appeal of communism to the disillusioned intellectuals at the end of World War II.

But it doesn't follow that communism rules mostly by winning the minds of men. Within the Soviet Union itself, it is difficult to appraise the people's feeling about their communist rulers. It must be remembered that Russia is the one country in which during the second world war, a great army, Vlasov's, went over to the enemy. It is the one country whose rulers so feared opposition in an entire region that they broke up four of their autonomous areas, deporting the people or their leaders to remote regions. Until very recently they were practicing genocide in the little Baltic countries which they had annexed by force.

It is hard to believe that a regime can be popular in a country in which millions of citizens are confined in slave camps. Doubt about the internal strength and assurance of the communist high command in the USSR was strengthened by the extraordinary nature of its announcement of Stalin's death and by events thereafter. Here was a regime which had been in power for thirty-five years. It had inculcated reverence for Stalin as semidivine. Yet in announcing Stalin's death, his successors issued a call to maintain "the steellike unity and monolithic unity in the ranks of the Party . . . to guard the unity of the Party as the apple of their eye . . . to educate all communists and working people to high political vigilance, intolerance and firmness in the struggle against internal and external enemies."

This call to unity was repeated hourly all through the day of March 6. Shortly before midnight the Party chiefs announced their conclusion that "the most important task of the Party and the government is to ensure uninterrupted and correct leadership of the entire life of the country

which demands the greatest unity of leadership and prevention of any kind of disorder and panic." The official announcement continued by proclaiming the necessity of
making at once a sweeping series of changes in personnel
and organizational structure of the leading Party and government bodies, changes which undid the personnel and
structural arrangements made less than five months earlier
by the nineteenth congress of the Communist Party under
personal direction of the Supreme Leader, who was now
not yet dead twenty-four hours.

Such extraordinary conduct on the death of an allegedly "beloved" leader argues an inner sense of insecurity
on the part of the government, a curious lack of confidence
in its own legitimacy, latent division in its ranks, and distrust of the popular reaction of the people, whose lives the
communist hierarchy sought "completely to control." *
How utterly different was the reaction of the government
and people in America at the death of Franklin Roosevelt!

Events following Stalin's death reveal a dictatorship
intent on preserving its fundamental power but constrained
to appease discontent by certain concessions inside the
USSR as well as in the satellite states. There is, for instance,
a well-publicized effort to make more consumers' goods
available. Whether these concessions will allay smoulder-
ing discontent; whether they mark a gradual beginning of
a slow evolution of communism away from Stalinist rig-

* See on this, "The Struggle for the Soviet Succession" by Bertram D.
Wolfe (*Foreign Affairs*, July, 1953), to which I am indebted.

ors; whether they are temporary accompaniments to the maneuvers inside the communist hierarchy for power; whether, whatever the intention of the rulers, these concessions will conciliate the masses or, after the usual historical precedent, whet their appetite for more—these and other questions can only be answered by time and events.

While one cannot trust Russian statistics, there seems to be no doubt that over-all production has increased sharply in recent years. Some of it may well be diverted to consumers' goods, thereby raising the general standard of living. The communist government has the prestige of victory in war and, until recently, successful aggrandizement since the war. It has no well-established democratic tradition with which to contend. It has manipulated wholesale its own mass culture for more than a generation. It has indoctrinated the people through the police force, radio, press, and schools as no nation was ever indoctrinated. Revolt won't be easy.

The situation in the satellite states is quite different. The June, 1953 risings in East Germany, paralleled to an unknown extent in other European satellites, were tremendously heartening evidences that no military tyranny can absolutely crush the passion of the masses for freedom and justice. Prior to these risings, and since, the steady stream of refugees—Germans, Czechs, and Poles—who, loving their ancestral homes, took the enormous risks of flight, has given eloquent evidence of communist failure— evidence that has not been sufficiently respected in the rest

of Europe. (In the summer of 1953 in Europe and Britain,
I was impressed with the wishful thinking of those who
were far more anxious to believe in the sincerity of the
Kremlin's very dubious peace campaign than in the evidence June 17 gave of hatred of communism by those who
know it best.)

When I considered the East German risings I remembered what Moshe Pijade, a high Yugoslav official and the-
oretician, had told me in 1951. He had expressed a tolerable
confidence that Yugoslavia might escape full-scale war
because Stalin would not involve Russian troops and because he would be afraid to push his satellite armies into
battle, since one military reverse might lead to mutiny
against the Russian high command.

In no area in Europe have the victories of communism
and the expansion of its territories since the close of World
War II been due to the voluntary acceptance of communist
doctrine and practice by the majority of the people. But
indigenous communist parties are still making disquieting
progress in Italy and France. A final judgment on the communist appeal in Europe is yet to be written.

Concerning China, it is even more difficult to pass
judgment. I thought I knew too much about communism
ever to believe that the Chinese communists were merely
agrarian reformers. Nevertheless, the testimony was overwhelming that on the way to power these communists
fought real evils with apparent devotion to the people's
interest. Once in power, they have, if anything, improved

on Russian techniques of brainwashing. But at the same time they have brought to bear upon the Chinese situation a new dynamism. They are rapidly introducing the modern technology which may sometime raise the standard of Chinese living. They have apparently less organized resistance on the Chinese mainland than any government for generations. They have made China in the eyes of its people and of most Asians a major power by the strength they have shown at home and in the Korean war. American ignorance of Asian problems and American blunders doubtless contributed to communist victory over Chiang. The latter under American prodding has belatedly established on Formosa a government superior in human values to that on the mainland. But what has happened in China was a social revolution not to be explained in terms of American blunderers or villains. The factors behind that type of social revolution still operate to a greater or less degree all over Asia.

In southeast Asia, Indonesia, and Africa, the imperialistic power was never Russia. It was the nations we call democratic which held millions of Asians and Africans in colonial subjection. Different as are the peoples of Asia, they have in common a history with little or no tradition of liberty, an experience of Western imperialism, a feudalistic social order, and an economy until very recently little benefited by modern technological advances. At the close of World War II, an overcrowded Asia had less food than a hundred years before.

Into this situation come the communist missionaries saying something like this: "As you now are, so yesterday was China. So the day before was Russia itself, predominantly a peasant nation, in economic if not political subjection to the West. Now look at the power of mighty China and remember that it was only communism which enabled the Chinese to lift themselves up out of the dominion of native landlords and usurers and foreign exploiters."

These communist missionaries have a definite line. Young people taken to Russia or China for education come back as disciplined agents of a secular church; and they are willing while on the road to power to live like the people among whom they work. By the very nature of democracy, the young people brought to America cannot be so indoctrinated and disciplined, and they come back somewhat accustomed to a higher standard of life than the peasants and artisans of Asian villages and overcrowded cities can enjoy.

It is perhaps not surprising, therefore, that more than once in India men said to me: "We don't like communism, but India will have to go communist. Only so can we be disciplined for industrialism and made to accumulate capital out of our already hungry stomachs." Here was no mention of individual freedom and no burning desire for it. It is always necessary for the lover of civil liberty to reflect that men seek to escape freedom as well as to win it; that they are interested not so much in the abstract freedom as in particular freedoms, of which the group freedom called national independence is at the moment the dearest in Asia.

Communist propaganda pretty well obscures the real fact of the nature of its rule, and I personally found it difficult to get educated Asians to believe how destitute of liberty was life behind the iron curtain. When I spoke of communist imperialism and illustrated my statement by pointing to Czechoslovakia, I was told in Japan and Indonesia: "But Asia is different."

Surely the liberal who wants to condone the record of communism in the field of liberty can find no support in this account of the reasons behind its undeniable appeal in Asian lands outside the iron curtain. At the same time, in my experience it is not true that Asians are so indifferent to liberty that they can never be moved at all by evidence of communist oppression. The Chinese communities which are so powerful a factor of life in Malaya, Thailand, and Indonesia have cooled in their enthusiasm for the communist government in Peking because of the way their relatives have been treated at home in an effort to extort money from the prosperous Chinese in other lands.

At no point in the world—except in Tito's Yugoslavia —is there any evidence of any change in the essential nature of communism. Tactics may be changing, but there is little evidence of any abatement of communism's drive for universal power over the bodies, and minds, and souls of men.

That statement is emphatically true of the nature of the communist movement within the United States—a subject so important to this book that it deserves a special chapter.

IV.

American Communism
and Liberty

FOR THE PURPOSES of this discussion, it becomes necessary to examine the history of communism in the United
States with reference to three interrelated questions. First,
how much power and influence has communism been able
to achieve in the United States? Second, how has it been
possible in this land of relative freedom to acquire power
so inimical to freedom? Third, how rigorous is the Party's
or the movement's control over its members and adherents?

We cannot be certain of statistics on communist
strength. J. Edgar Hoover has put membership in the Party
today at about 21,000. At its height, it was between 70,000
and 100,000. Mr. Hoover is probably correct in estimating
ten fellow travelers or persons strongly influenced by communism for every communist. The Party's voting strength

was always of secondary importance, and the turnover in its membership very large.

Although by any test communist strength is at a low ebb today in the United States, it is by no means so negligible as some optimists affirm. There is a communist press in English and some foreign languages. Communists still dominate seven unions with a total membership of between 300,000 and 400,000. One communist controls labor in copper and zinc mines; another, communications workers in Western Union; another, a considerable segment of the electrical and electronics industry. Harry Bridges' union is very powerful in Hawaii and on the West Coast. An excellent staff report to the subcommittee on labor and labor-management relations of the Senate's Committee on Labor and Public Welfare, Eighty-second Congress, second session, presents an important case history in the tactics of communist unionism in the Marine Cooks and Stewards Union. I find numerous evidences of quiet and misinformed sympathy for communism in the country, much of it a direct reaction to McCarthyist tactics.

There were two periods when communist interpenetration of government service, some of it at a high level, was very considerable. The first period was between the inauguration of Stalin's policy of a united front against fascism at the end of 1934 and his pact with Hitler in August 1939; the second, following Hitler's attack on Stalin, was the period of our own participation in World War II. At this time communists were among the most vociferous of

patriots and there is no question that their influence in
unions was exerted on the side of the government to prevent strikes. Communist patriotism at home and American
admiration for the valor of our communist ally, Russia, in
the war, carried over after V-E day. The honeymoon lasted
in considerable strength until the Czechoslovak coup on
February 25, 1948. As late as the summer of 1948, the communists, while definitely in a minority in Henry Wallace's
Progressive Party, by their disciplined skill and experience
controlled the convention which nominated him and
drafted most of Wallace's campaign speeches.

I have been told that it is incorrect to say that the communists controlled the Progressive Party in 1948, since Wallace himself was not a communist and the platform did not
champion communism. This sort of statement ignores a
basic fact about communist procedure. What communists
may advocate at a specific time often has little to do with
the ultimate program of communism. It has everything to
do with the supposed popular appeal of the program. Communists under Moscow's direction are sailors who may
take long and unexpected tacks but never forget the loca-
tion of the finish line in their race for power.

The Progressive Party in 1948 was only the most conspicuous of the communist fronts. We shall later have to
say more about the Attorney General's list of subversive
organizations or of organizations controlled by communists
and used by communists as "fronts" or "transmission belts."
These front organizations are not much used in countries

where communist parties are strong, but they serve communist ends in America and some other countries where the Party itself is numerically weak. The nominal reason for creating a front in the thirties was to deal with a specific problem, the menace of war and fascism, for instance. The diligent communists who set up the front (or interpenetrated one already existing) used it for contacts and to enhance their prestige. If they dominated the front sufficiently, they raised money for the party in the name of the front.

The current Attorney General's list itself is open to criticism. The lists compiled by state authorities are worse. Worst of all is the use of these lists as infallible guides for blacklisting everybody ever connected with any of the groups named on them. Nevertheless, to my own knowledge, most of the organizations on the Attorney General's list were started or captured by the communists. Often innocent members were unaware of the process of capture and control. It is probable that most Americans belong to one or more organizations that could be dominated by an energetic, firmly disciplined minority.

The communist policy of the united front in the late thirties and the general emotional atmosphere among liberals made interpenetration easy. The communists often championed very good causes for their own ends. Their interpenetration of labor unions would never have succeeded except that in organizing campaigns and in strikes, the communists and those whom they controlled usually did a good job for labor, *for the time being,* especially in the united-front period after 1935. In an earlier period, more than once they had sacrificed the interests of organized labor as such in a strike situation to the particular line of the Party. This was notably true in the textile strike led by Fred Beal in Gastonia, North Carolina, in 1929.

It is very hard to say how much communist interpenetration accomplished in influencing government policy. But unquestionably communists or their close fellow travelers won high and responsible posts. The report of the Jenner Committee released on August 24, 1953 is, thanks to Robert Morris, its attorney, a sober and well-documented statement on Soviet spy rings inside the United States government. Its charges against individuals admittedly fall short, in many cases, of legal proof, but they are well supported. Says the report:

> According to the evidence in our records, those involved in the secret Communist underground included
>> an executive assistant to the President of the United States;
>> an Assistant Secretary of the Treasury;
>> the Director of the Office of Special Political Affairs for the State Department;
>> the Secretary of the International Monetary Fund;
>> the head of the Latin-American Division of the Office of Strategic Services;
>> a member of the National Labor Relations Board;
>> secretary of the National Labor Relations Board;
>> chief counsel, Senate Subcommittee on Civil Liberties;

chief, Statistical Analysis Branch, War Production Board;

Treasury Department representative and adviser in Financial Control Division of the North African Economic Board in UNRRA (United Nations Relief and Rehabilitation Administration) and at the meeting of the Council of Foreign Ministers in Moscow;

director, National Research Project of the Works Progress Administration.

There was definitely a strong pro-communist or at least pro-Russian group in the State Department, but for the most part it comprised men who seem never to have been under definite communist direction or control. George Kennan, who opposed the pro-Russian group in the State Department, stated in a speech in Scranton, before the Pennsylvania Bar Association, that in his judgment communists and fellow travelers were not responsible for any important policy decision in foreign affairs. I think this is true of the Morgenthau Plan for Germany even if Harry Dexter White had a large part in its authorship.

It has always been my opinion that the responsibility was Roosevelt's. He seems to have been constitutionally incapable of understanding a "true believer" like Stalin. His dealings with Russia indicate that, at least until shortly before the end of his life, Roosevelt thought Stalin was just another Georgia politician—perhaps a little more ornery than usual because he came from Georgia, USSR, instead of Georgia, USA, but, nevertheless, in the long run manageable, with the right sort of handling and compromises. The most that can be said of the communists' comparative success in interpenetration of the government is that they got into positions where they could be very useful to their party and their cause, at least as long as Stalin's line did not involve frontal conflict with our government. I think that they did not so much determine foreign or domestic policy as push the administration along a road it wanted to travel.

Espionage is, of course, a different matter. On the record of American communism, by June 1, 1953, there were eighteen one-time Communist Party members and sympathizers who had confessed espionage activities, four who had been convicted without confessing, eight who had been convicted of lesser crimes for which they had been indicted as a result of investigation into alleged espionage activity, and five convicted of lesser crimes not involving the charge of espionage activity.

This is not a record to be ignored. Unquestionably, the atomic spy ring of which the most important member was Klaus Fuchs in England greatly facilitated Russian development of atomic bombs. It may be that the documents which Julian Henry Wadleigh admitted taking from the State Department files, or the documents which Alger Hiss denied taking, were not themselves of great importance. They were taken at a time when fascism rather than communism was the aggressive totalitarian force in world affairs. Nevertheless, we have clear proof that men in responsible positions, under communist influence and direction, felt justified in violating all the usual canons of good faith and loyalty in the positions which they held. At the most favorable interpretation, they set up their judgment, a judgment formed under communist influence or discipline, over the well-established rules of moral conduct. In so doing Alger Hiss did a harm to civil liberties unequaled by any man in American history. Since his conviction, it has been impossible to argue that we do not have to worry about communism. The invariable answer is: "Ah, but what about Alger Hiss?" He was the kind of young American, it had seemed, whom every mother wanted her son to be, yet it turned out that he had been a secret communist, guilty of espionage for Russia.

That brings us to our second question: How was it possible that so many apparently high-grade Americans became communists and so many more so tolerant of communism? Here the answer is more difficult to give. But the lines which a fuller answer might follow are not hard to indicate. To a large extent the reasons in America were the same as in Europe. They were both psychological and historical. Triumphant communism in Russia grew out of successful revolution against a czarist regime which all liberal Americans despised for its crimes against liberty. The earliest critics of Lenin, Trotsky, and their movement were too often themselves reactionaries, deeply self-interested in the old order for economic or political reasons, and careless of the truth. The struggle of the victorious western allies against the emerging Soviet power was not to be justi-

fied as sound ethics or sound politics. It was damned by its
feebleness. The fact that it was attempted at all contributed
greatly to a sense of guilt, which grew rapidly among many
Americans following the first world war. We were bitterly
disillusioned about the outcome of the war to make the
world safe for democracy and about the quality of our own
democracy, which in the immediate postwar period had
been deeply discredited by race riots and the rise of the
Ku Klux Klan.

The hectic and speculative prosperity of the Coolidge
period on the whole added to the sense of guilt among a
few of the more sensitive among the rich and the comfort-
able. In the twenties, with the subsidence of the hysteria
of the war and immediate postwar period, the American
public generally was disinclined to play cops and robbers
with the communists or anybody else. The communists
were "persecuted" just enough to enable them to exploit
a rather cheap and easy type of martyrdom. But in no way
were they suppressed.*

Then came the great depression. And to thousands of
Americans who would now like to forget it, it looked as if
Russia had found an answer to depression and unemployment which American capitalism had missed. The communists themselves, although comparatively few in number,
were active in behalf of the unemployed. By energy and

* Of the four or five major cases involving communists between the
time of the Gitlow case and Pearl Harbor, in only one, the case of Anita
Whitney, was the final appeal lost. She was convicted under a California
law in 1927.

discipline, they managed to get a high degree of control in various WPA projects, particularly those designed to help writers and artists. Socialists around New York were often the victims of communist control at important levels of activity.

Then came the united-front period, in which fascism was the great enemy of all liberals. It obviously gave the communists a great chance to advance their cause. If it had not been for the Russian purges beginning in 1936, communists might possibly have captured all the more aggressive sections of the labor movement and all the organizations of antifascist liberals.

To be sure, most of those whom the communists manipulated in labor and liberal movements and whose tolerance, if not approval, they won, showed no sign of joining the Communist Party or becoming disciplined adherents of it. But many did. Once the communist church was established on the world stage, it was a conspicuously obvious refuge for Americans revolting against old and stuffy authorities, race prejudice, and economic injustice. It was easy emotionally for all sorts of young people with private rebellions and frustrations to join the Party. Morris Ernst and David Loth in their *Report on the American Communist* have made a good beginning of a case study of the reasons why many young Americans joined the Party and why so many of them were soon disillusioned and left it. (Jules Monnerot's study of the *Psychology and Sociology of Communism,* to which I have already referred, is a deeper and

more profound analysis of psychological forces which
swept many men, not necessarily exceptional Americans,
into the secular religion of communism.) It was a movement which in the thirties seemed to thousands of young
Americans to satisfy what are—but only superficially—op-
posite desires. It appealed to men wanting power, power
within the Party and power collectively for the Party. It
appealed to men, sometimes the same men, who wanted
discipline and craved support, even the support of communist chains.

The great reverse in communist fortunes has been due
far less to the zeal of the McCarthys, big or little, far less
to the stupidities of those who still attack communism for
what it is not, a doctrine of economic equality, or to the
self-interested malice of those who use the communist stick
to beat the socialist and liberal dog, than to the record communism has made inside Russia and the crimes of its imperialistic aggression. There was tremendous disillusion-
ment in the spectacle of a secular religion in America so
completely under the control of a communist pope who
is also the chief of a mighty empire that its devotees overnight had to learn to bless that which the day before they
had cursed. Among the worst of McCarthyist stupidities
is insistence on making communism, for however short a
time professed, an unforgivable sin or one from which re-
demption can be purchased only by turning informer.

There are honest liberals who will admit virtually all
that I have been saying and yet continue to doubt whether

the American Communist Party is really completely controlled from Moscow or, if it is, whether its ordinary rank and file of members feel the weight of that control. It is, of course, true that for prudential reasons the American Communist Party announced formally its withdrawal from the Comintern before it was dissolved by Stalin during the war. But it is also true that no communist leader and no communist publication has ever knowingly criticized the Kremlin. The record of the Kremlin's assertion of control was publicly written by a series of three events:

1. On the inauguration of the Third International, the American Socialist Party considered membership in it. Lenin imposed twenty-one "points," two of which demanded changes in the American leadership which the Socialist Party would not accept. It was then rejected. The Communist International demanded total obedience.

2. In 1926, Jay Lovestone and other leaders of what was clearly then the majority of the Communist Party in America were directed to report to Moscow and were then ordered by Stalin himself to become a minority—a minority absolutely obedient even in thought to the line dictated to the new majority created by Stalin's fiat. He himself made Earl Browder chief of the Party in the United States.

3. Later Stalin himself, through the mouth of the Frenchman Duclos, repudiated the line which in Stalin's interest Browder and the whole American Communist Party had followed after Pearl Harbor. Browder's comrades, who had docilely voted with him, turned upon him

with contumely and abuse which was a frightening expression of the psychology of communist obedience. During
the intervening years, the communists had been compelled,
on the signing of the Hitler-Stalin pact, to abandon the
united-front line and denounce the imperialist warmakers
of the west. And then with equal speed after Hitler's attack on Stalin, they swung to support the war they had
opposed, and demanded an immediate second front by a
military establishment which they had made attempts to
weaken.

When one speaks of communist discipline, one does
not assert that at all times and with equal compulsions it is
laid heavily upon the communists. There were doubtless
long periods in the experience of the average communist
when he was not required to do much except to attend
meetings, pay dues, and talk up his cause among his friends.
But always in communist theory, he who accepted the
secular religion was at its absolute disposal. It was from
the ranks of idealists that undercover operators for communism were recruited.* Quotations to establish the extent of this control are many. They can be illustrated by the
following instructions to teachers from the official organ
of the Communist Party, *The Communist*, of May, 1937,
as quoted by Sidney Hook:

> Party and Y.C.L. (Young Communist League) frac-
> tions set up within classes and departments must supple-
> ment and combat by means of discussions, brochures,

* See on this the report of the Canadian Royal Commission.

etc., bourgeois omissions and distortions in the regular curriculum. . . . Marxist-Leninist analysis must be injected into every class.

Communist teachers must take advantage of their positions, without exposing themselves, to give their students to the best of their ability working class education.

To enable the teachers in the party to do the latter, the party must take careful steps to see that all teacher comrades are given thorough education in the teaching of Marxism-Leninism. Only when teachers have really mastered Marxism-Leninism will they be able skillfully to inject it into their teaching at the least risk of exposure and at the same time conduct struggles around the schools in a truly Bolshevik manner.

The Communist Party from its early beginnings has had a control commission to check upon the activities of members and expel those who disobey instructions. For years, the Communist Party actually published the list of members whom it had disciplined. Earl Browder, in one of his numerous hearings before a congressional committee, under questioning testified as follows:

MR. MATTHEWS: In numerous instances we have a notation [of the Central Control Commission] that the expelled member "refused to carry out decisions." That is in line with your explanation of the relationship between the Communist Party of the United States and the Comintern?

MR. BROWDER: Exactly.

MR. MATTHEWS: A member must carry out all decisions of the party or be expelled from the party?

THE CHAIRMAN: Is that correct?

MR. BROWDER: Yes, that is correct.

MR. STARNES: A party member does not have any latitude or discretion in the matter—he has to carry out orders?

MR. BROWDER: The party [member] has to carry out orders.*

Evidence given in investigations in 1952 shows that this control commission or its equivalent still exists and operates. Kalinin in a speech to the Fourteenth Congress of the Communist Party in 1925 stated a principle of universal application in the Communist Party: "The idea that the truth remains the truth is admissible in a philosophical club, but in the Party, the decisions of the congress are obligatory also upon those who doubt the correctness of a decision. . . . Our Party is strong through the fact that the decisions of the majority are obligatory upon all not only in form, but in substance." A few years later Stalin substituted himself for the Congress as supreme over communists, and the American Communist Party accepted that rule just as it now accepts the rule of Malenkov and Co.

Such are the facts which led the Board of Directors of the American Civil Liberties Union, often charged with softness toward communists, to approve by almost unanimous vote the following categorical statement in the spring of 1953:

* Hearings before Special Committee on Un-American Activities, House of Representatives, Seventy-sixth Congress, first session, on House Res. 282, Vol. 7, p. 4417.

The ACLU holds that the American Communist Party is distinctively and essentially characterized both by extreme anti-democratic doctrine and practice and by obedience to the government of the Soviet Union, a despotic foreign power which dominates a world-wide revolutionary movement unprecedentedly threatening the national independence and individual civil liberties of all other countries. It is thus sharply differentiated from traditional American political parties, and all its present adherents are to some degree involved in its distinctive and essential character.

V.

What Should We Have Done?

WE CANNOT DEFEND liberty by denying the danger of the organized communist conspiracy even if at the moment it is weak within the United States. It was a serious liberal error, contributing to the rise of McCarthyism, that so many liberals so long minimized the communist evil. Communism is a monstrous threat to any valid theory or practice of freedom and fellowship among men. It jeopardizes all that is best in our American way of life and imperils even our existence as an independent nation.

Obviously the chief danger to us at present is from abroad. It is communism in control of two mighty empires and their satellites which threatens the freedom and peace of mankind. The struggle against it is centered mainly in our foreign policy; it involves the arms race and the cold war.

But communism within the United States was once a fairly powerful fifth column for Stalin, and its present weakness is not so great as to make its direct value to the Kremlin negligible. Communism has occasioned the rise of McCarthyism. That answer to it is, at the moment and inside our boundaries, a more widespread challenge to the Jeffersonian ideal than communism; by its consequences, it operates in the long run as a kind of sixth column in support of Stalin's successors. It too must be fought.

In this double struggle there are unfortunately some avowed liberals who aid both McCarthyism and communism by persistently minimizing the danger of communism in America and by assuming that because the complex of ideas and actions which we sometimes call McCarthyism is bad on the whole, therefore none of its elements is necessary or even defensible; and because the McCarthys, big and little, have given the wrong answer to communism, there is no need for any answer except a touching faith that truth is mighty and must prevail. Not so can our freedom be preserved and expanded.

In our effort to meet the challenge which communism (and other conspiratorial movements) present to the Jeffersonian ideal, I think that we shall get further by ignoring McCarthyism for the time being and asking ourselves what action rational citizens should have commended—what they should now commend—to their government in the face of the communist war on freedom. Under democracy, to what liberties are men and women entitled who, in power, would deny all freedom? The Jeffersonian faith in the power of truth was postulated on its ability to prevail over error, openly advocated in the market place of ideas.

What about the error which is advanced by a conspiratorial organization, an organization which instructs its adherents wherever possible to mask their true allegiance? That allegiance in the final analysis must be given not only to a theory of communism but to an international organization whose supreme leader is also the head of a foreign power already engaged in cold war with our own country. Herein, rather than in its advocacy of future revolutionary force and violence, lies the real danger of communism and its essential difference from other radical or protest movements in American history.

It is exceedingly doubtful if William Z. Foster, present leader of American communism, ever advocated more revolutionary force and violence—if as much—as the physical force preached by anarchists of the years before World War I. But they, like all previous varieties of American radicals and rebels, were flamboyantly honest. The abolitionists, Populists, socialists, and IWW's shouted their beliefs. The wobblies helped their imprisoned comrades in struggles against local police authorities by flocking to fill the jails. Mr. Foster, following the steel strike of 1919, of which he was the leader, desired support from socialists and others, myself among them, for plans he had for organizing labor.

Repeatedly he assured me that he was not a communist or under communist control. He only acknowledged his communist convictions when he was arrested in connection with a big secret meeting in Bridgeton, Michigan, in the summer of 1922.* Obviously government and people have a different problem in dealing with the communist William Z. Foster and his Party than it had with Emma Goldman, the anarchist, and her friends.

It is the conspiratorial nature of communism in pursuit of its objective of supreme power over us which necessitates surveillance. To the man who openly boasts that he will save the world by making us robots or slaves we can well afford to prove the strength of freedom by letting him rant —save, perhaps, in specific emergencies presenting clear and present dangers. But the man who talks and acts in conspiratorial secrecy to achieve his party's objective presents an unknown danger which government must discover and, at the very least, expose to the light.

On the record of American communism, as we have already set that record forth, and of the crimes committed in its name, the government was and is obligated to keep it under the active watchfulness of the FBI. The offenses already proved to have been committed by communists awaken reasonable suspicion of other similar activities inspired and directed by this conspiratorial movement. Thomas Jefferson himself would be among the first to admit

* This case, brought under a Michigan criminal syndicalist law, was never brought to final trial.

that laws against subversive acts, including espionage and sabotage, and their rigorous enforcement, violate no principle or precept of the Bill of Rights. He would probably also admit, however sorrowfully, that special provisions must be made to ascertain the loyalty and reliability of persons in positions to injure their country through espionage, sabotage, or plain carelessness.

But high government officials, the FBI, congressional investigating committees, and plain citizens in their efforts to discover subversion and drag conspiracy into the open are under imperative obligation, as Sidney Hook has ably insisted, sharply to distinguish between heresy, or dissent from popularly accepted belief, and conspiracy—an obligation sadly ignored in practice. In logic and on the historical record the outspoken dissenter is not the conspirator or the close associate of conspirators. Even within the communist movement there has been a conscious attempt to keep the open spokesmen as far as possible in ignorance of underground activity. One reason that Louis Budenz, once an open and acknowledged communist editor, has given the authorities so little important and trustworthy information after his renunciation of communism is probably the fact that the major leaders deliberately kept him, the editor and propagandist, from knowing much more than the scuttle-butt talk or gossip from which not even conspiratorial groups are free.

A political dissenter may now and then talk like a communist on certain issues. He can hardly help it when the communist line on many issues has been shifted so often and so sharply. More often it is the ill-informed patriot who discovers a false identity of heresy with communism on the assumption that communism is everything that he doesn't like or understand. Responsible authorities imperil liberty without catching communist (or fascist) subversives if and when they confuse heresy with conspiracy.

Responsible authorities—and plain citizens—are under a second obligation in forming their judgments. They must allow for the fact that men can and do change their minds, in particular that what men thought and said at a given period of history—say the early thirties—may be very different from what they think today. The notion that there is no such thing as a repentant communist or communist sympathizer unless he turns public informer is notoriously contrary to fact. J. Edgar Hoover, chief of the FBI, and others have estimated that there are in America between 700,000 and 1,000,000 ex-members or disciplined adherents of communism. This subject will be discussed again when McCarthyism is considered. But it should be said now that a proper evaluation of time and circumstance is essential to discriminate appraisal of men and women charged with communist allegiance.

But after these things have been said, the question remains: What rights should communists still loyal to the Party possess under our theory of freedom? Here are five answers which I think stand the test of examination:

1. Communists as individuals are entitled to that due

process of law which our Constitution and laws guarantee
to men charged with the most ignoble crimes. There is
nothing in the nature of communism or the magnitude of
the internal threat from communism to excuse, much less
justify, star-chamber proceedings, or any abrogation of
the rights which have been developed under the concept
of due process of law.

By the same token, the communists are entitled to the
same protection of freedom of speech and of the press as
regards their public utterances as applies to the rest of us.
If in public speech they advocate or seem to advocate violent or subversive action, the question of clear and immediate danger must be raised before their conviction.

2. Covert, as contrasted with open, speech, that is,
speech within a conspiratorial organization, should not fall
under the full protection which the First Amendment gives
to open, public speech and discussion. I am much impressed
by Morris Ernst's constitutional argument on this point (in
the *Columbia Law Review,* May, 1953) and his conclu-
sions in terms of public policy. The policy he proposes
would

> (1) Protect all private and secret speech regarding the
> advisability of changes in government . . . so long as
> such discussion does not involve the "overt act" neces-
> sary to establish any criminal conspiracy. (2) In the
> event that, as a result of private and secret speech, any
> one or more persons were to undertake any activity
> toward an unlawful end, the speech could not be pro-
> tected any more than would a bank robbers' conference.

The overt act in furtherance of such a criminal conspiracy need not, of course, be criminal itself.

Mr. Ernst believes that there is a three-fold advantage to this legal distinction between secret and public speech:

First by clearly distinguishing a secret speech from the kind of open public discussion which the First Amendment was designed to protect, we may minimize the possibility that the strength of the First Amendment may be diluted with respect to the open speech which is the basis of effective democratic government. Secondly, by applying the "overt act" test to secret speech, secret speech absent overt acts will come under no restriction whatever—an end desirable in itself if the preservation of our form of government is not to be achieved at the price of undue invasion of privacy or exchange of ideas. Thirdly, by granting First Amendment protection to public speech and not to secret speech, ideas will be further invited into the general public market place where they may be subjected to public ridicule and debate, and where they may be accepted or rejected without resort to violence.

3. Despite the conspiratorial nature of the communist movement, the Communist Party should not be outlawed. This is a judgment not deduced from the Bill of Rights so much as from considerations of sound public policy. The Communist Party, that part of the communist movement which holds conventions, adopts platforms, nominates or endorses candidates, is engaged in a legitimate and essential feature of our democratic way of life. Necessarily it is doing certain things openly; its statements and its candi-

dates can be judged by the electorate as they judge those of other parties. It is basic to our democracy that it provide an orderly way for men to make changes, even changes by their nature revolutionary. Only so are we Americans able to say to voters: "We offer in the ballot not only an alternative to the bullet for achieving change, but one vastly less self-defeating in obtaining desirable results." That means that we must scrupulously protect the right of men to form radical parties and in them advocate their cause and seek support. To outlaw the communist or any other party engaged in legitimate political activities, however objectionable its program may seem to a majority, is to deny a basic democratic principle and invite subversive and ultimately violent action in place of the political action which the government has outlawed.

The evidence in various court procedures and the statements of former communists makes it plain that the men and women actively engaged in subversive activities or espionage are always withdrawn from activity in the Communist Party; they and their work are unknown to rank-and-file members. The outlawry of the Party might possibly make it a little more difficult to find and recruit underground workers, although that's not certain. What is certain is that the outlawry of the Party would make it far harder, not only for the public but even for the FBI, to keep tabs on communist thought and activity; it would make it easier for communists to practice deceit. As long as there is an open and legal Communist Party there must be avowed communists to run it. The existence of the Party to some extent provides, almost automatically, the "disclosure" which the McCarran Act clumsily seeks. In the familiar illustration, it is the part of the iceberg above water which shows where the danger really lurks.

In practice the outlawry of the Party would give communism the appeal of both mystery and martyrdom to thousands of Americans, especially American youth. It would further encourage determined and intelligent communists to interpenetrate other parties—even the Republican!—or under some circumstances to form a new party with an innocuous name and, outwardly, a legitimate program.

Finally, the outlawry of the Communist Party would discredit American democracy abroad and add to the suspicion of us which already hampers our foreign policy. Communism in many European countries is too strong to be outlawed by existing governments. The attempt might invite serious riots, if not rebellion; it would certainly recoil on the government. Other nations, like Great Britain, would regard outlawry of a Communist Party as preposterous. For us Americans to do what other democracies won't or can't do would bring upon us contempt for hysteria rather than respect for strength.

4. What we should not do directly we should not do indirectly. If it is unsound policy to outlaw the Communist Party by direct legislation, it is at least equally unsound to accomplish the same end by laying upon it requirements

impossible of fulfillment (as does the McCarran Internal
Security Act) or by sending successive waves of its leaders
to jail by trials under the Smith Act. These laws will be
examined in connection with the discussion of McCarthyism. Here it is important to insist that outlawry of the Communist Party must not be sought by indirect but effective
means allegedly directed to other ends.

5. The rights of communists to stay out of jail, to speak
openly for their cause, to organize their own open party
and participate in elections, do not imply an equivalent
right to seek and hold every sort of office in a democratic
state (or in democratic unions). To be sure, if communists
are to exist as members of the normal community they must
have a right to work. But not at tasks or in public positions
where they may, under orders, practice a type of espionage,
sabotage, or subversion which might jeopardize the republic. No such right exists in common sense or in the Bill of
Rights. Today there is little disposition among liberals to
deny that there are "sensitive positions" in government
service—and some types of private employment—which
communists should not hold. The dispute concerns the
number and nature of positions to be regarded as "sensitive" and the methods to be employed to ascertain loyalty
and trustworthiness. These problems will be considered
after the examination of McCarthyism. But, forgetting Mc-
Carthyism for a moment, there exist two important problems in this area raised by the nature of communism itself.
The first question is: Should communists be employed in

the field of communication through radio, television, and moving pictures, and on the stage? If so, under what conditions? The second concerns the right of communists to teach in schools and colleges.

The first question is simpler than the second. A play, a radio or television script, the performance of an actor, can be judged by itself and on its own merits regardless of the general beliefs of writer or actor. That communication is necessarily out in the open. No secret conspiracy can be carried out through it. The world would be culturally impoverished if artists, musicians, writers and actors had all to be screened for character, respectability, and opinion. The difficulty in this field arises from the extension of the right of a communist or suspected communist to be judged on performance to the right of a communist to preferred employment just because he is suspect, in order to rebuke censorship. I have listened to arguments which would seem to insist not only that Hollywood moguls must not reject actors or writers because they are communists or communist sympathizers, but that they must employ them even if they prefer others capable of at least equally good work. (Incidentally, in the days of their strength, communists in Hollywood managed effectually to close many doors of employment to anticommunist writers and artists. It was this fact that might have justified a proper sort of legislative inquiry into Hollywood affairs.)

The question of the right of communists to teach in our schools and colleges is more difficult because it has proved hard to deal with communists without jeopardizing academic freedom. Some of these difficulties will be discussed later. But the principle seems plain. Communists have no right to teach, because in becoming Communist Party members or adherents they have performed an act of surrender of their own conscience and of their freedom to serve truth, an act which unfits them for their high task. To defend this surrender by saying that the teacher does not know the meaning and significance of his act is to indict him for intellectual incapacity which should debar him from teaching. Herein lies no charge of mere guilt by association, although it is legitimate to judge men's character and competence in part by their associations. What we attack is an act destructive of the very basis of democracy, the act of giving one's allegiance in thought and action to a conspiratorial organization, controlled by the rulers of a foreign power, which dictates what its adherents must believe in religion, science, politics, and philosophy. How can the man guilty of that act teach our children the basic principles of democracy? What right have we to risk them to his care?

It is an insult to our schools and the great function of the teaching profession to say that it doesn't matter that a teacher is a communist (or a fascist) so long as he can't be caught in a specific act of totalitarian indoctrination while he teaches spelling or arithmetic. It argues an ignorance of the pervasive influence of a teacher to say that he can do no harm to his pupils unless he specifically tries to teach them communism. Short of that, the devoted and able communist or fascist teacher living with his pupils in grade school can influence them in a dozen ways to reject the democratic approach to life in favor of attitudes more appropriate to communism or some other totalitarianism.

In the many debates on this subject to which I have listened, the supporters of the right of the communist to teach, subject only to discharge for proved indoctrination, have been compelled logically to extend the same right to Ku Kluxers, Nazis, or fascists. Yet, if the issue had first been raised against the Klansmen or the German Bundists, many of these liberals would have eagerly joined a crusade to purge our schools of such wholly undesirable teachers. And all of them habitually employ standards in choosing and retaining confidential secretaries which they would deny to educational authorities in our public schools!

They say in defense of communist teachers that probably most of them keep communism out of their classrooms, that they are better than their creed, that in practically no cases have communist teachers been ordered to inculcate disloyalty.

Fortunately, men are frequently better than their creeds; it is indeed doubtful if it has often suited communist tactics to order active sedition among teachers, or even the obvious inculcation of communism. Nevertheless, the act of a man or woman in surrendering to this external conspiratorial authority itself corrupts the proper teaching of the attitudes upon which the future of our democracy depends. And the instruction to communist activity (quoted in the previous chapter) has been widely obeyed. I was long enough a member of the Teachers Union (AFL) * in New York City when the communist caucus managed to run its affairs to know how false is the notion that most communist teachers don't try to do as they are instructed to further communism. Sidney Hook, in his book *Heresy, Yes —Conspiracy, No,* marshals abundant evidence to refute all defense of the harmlessness of communist teachers.†

To my mind, the problem of the communist teacher in the college or university is less serious than in the grade schools. Such a professor is not with immature pupils day in and day out. He works at a level and under conditions which permit discussion. If, therefore, he teaches in a field where the Kremlin has not laid down a line, and if he acknowledges his communism, I should not think him very dangerous. Nevertheless, the argument holds, and he teaches by exceptional permission and not by inherent right.

I have been dealing with an underlying principle. I am aware how difficult is the discovery of communism. I do not approve the clumsy laws and administrative procedures which have been invoked to save us from communism. They are doing more harm than good. They have hurt

* This union was later reorganized as the Teachers Guild. Pro-communist elements formed a Teachers Union in the CIO. It is now independent.

† See especially his chapter on "Communism and Academic Freedom."

the honest liberal or dissenter more than the communist. In general, I oppose burning down barns to catch rats; it is usually the horses that die. But I believe in catching rats. And I think there is law enough without so-called "witch-hunting" to enable our educational authorities to refuse to hire communists or to continue the employment of proved adherents to its antidemocratic doctrine and practice.

The application of this principle will require more discussion after the examination of the McCarthyist reaction and its threat to freedom. What has been done is very different from what should have been done.

VI.

McCarthyism and Liberty

IT HAS BEEN the fortune of Senator Joseph McCarthy, from the once progressive state of Wisconsin, to give his name to the complex of attitudes, procedures, and laws with which America most volubly confronts communism within her borders. It would be premature to say that McCarthyism has conquered our courts and our country; there are many heartening evidences to the contrary. It would be contrary to fact to hold the Senator solely responsible for McCarthyism. It is an even more serious historical error to credit him with the major measures taken by the federal government against subversion. Nevertheless, he has made himself in the public mind, here and abroad, and only less in official Washington itself, the symbol of militant opposition to insidious disloyalty. In searching out that evil he above all others is the Grand Inquisitor, he above all others the exponent of government by denunciation.

Most of the elements of McCarthyism long antedate the Senator's emergence to prominence. The sort of patriotism which is the last refuge of the scoundrel is a perversion of love of country for personal advantage far older than the crusty British Tory, Samuel Johnson, to whom we owe the definition. On a less self-interested plane this kind of patriotism identifies love of country with dislike of foreigners, love of conformity, and exaggerated suspicion of dissent. Specimens of it were to be found in certain resolutions of the American Legion, and in the even more prejudiced utterances of the Daughters of the American Revolution, years before Joe McCarthy terrorized his fellow senators and Republican associates by his identification of patriotism with respect for his fulminations.

Moreover, the Grand Inquisitor has profited by a falsehood which he did not invent and which others propagandize at great cost. That is the lie which identifies communism with democratic socialism and the welfare state, the lie which affirms that liberty is bound up with the right of private owners of the nation's mineral wealth and water power to exploit them for private profit. (Under our present tax laws we taxpayers bear most of the cost of our indoctrination in this falsehood, since great corporations deduct it as an advertising expense before paying their taxes.)

Not even the inquisitorial methods of McCarthyism were originated by the Senator. Liberals who passionately denounce them showed no equivalent concern for individual rights when New Dealers controlled the machinery of congressional inquiry. In the investigation of allegedly "un-American" activities Martin Dies set the pattern as chairman of the House Committee, first established in 1938. As a matter of fact, investigatorial procedures of the senatorial committees are today somewhat fairer—or less unfair—to the individual than were those of the House Committee under Dies. (Mr. Robert Morris, chief counsel for the McCarran, later the Jenner, Committee, deserves much of the credit for these improvements, but from time to time the McCarthy and Velde committees revert to the standards set by those good Democrats, Messrs. Dies and Rankin.) State committees, notably the "little Dies," or the Tenney, Committee in California, were worse than their federal models. The California inquisitor, Jack Tenney, had done his worst and passed over to open support of Gerald L. K. Smith, anti-Semitism and all, before McCarthy took command in Washington.

As for legislation and administrative procedures directed to the discovery and punishment of disloyalty, McCarthy had nothing to do with the passage of the Smith Act in 1940, and little to do with the McCarran Act of 1950. He had not begun his personal crusade against communism when President Truman instituted loyalty examinations for federal employees in 1947. He contributed nothing to the conviction of Alger Hiss. (But I have run across Americans who believe him responsible for it!)

It is not, however, true that McCarthy has failed to expose a single communist. A relatively small number of his sweeping charges have found legitimate targets. He has exposed some carelessness in loyalty inquiries. But not enough to make his investigatory work important to American security.

Why then the term "McCarthyism" and the general acceptance of the Senator as symbol of an anticommunism of universal suspicion of dissent? Partly, of course, because of McCarthy's skill as a demagogue; partly because he came along at the right time in a country somewhat disappointed in the consequences of its own attempts at international virtue, shocked by the world-wide impact of communist imperialism, and outraged by communist abuse of its confidence in Stalin as an ally. His publicity techniques made the press and radio unwittingly build him up.

The Senator successfully exploited anticommunism as a campaign issue in 1952; he is credited with important help in the campaigns of seven or eight of his colleagues. By the outrageous seniority system he became chairman of a permanent investigating committee in 1953. So his colleagues thought it safer to ignore the very serious questions about his own financial transactions which a Senate subcommittee had raised, questions which the Grand Inquisitor of others contemptuously refused to answer. Such success is unfortunately impressive.*

---

* On September 5, 1953, the Department of Justice announced that on the basis of material turned over by the Senate subcommittee, it found no legal grounds for prosecuting Senator McCarthy. No victim had appeared to complain of fraud or embezzlement; no law forbade a senator to accept a fee, nominally for a book, from a corporation like Lustron which had a deep interest in his actions as a member of a committee investigating

It is significant of the man, of the *ism,* and perhaps of the mind of "the Lonely Crowd" that McCarthy by no means began his public career as conservative or anticommunist. Originally, he was a Democrat. As a Republican in his campaign against Robert M. LaFollette, Jr., for the Republican senatorial nomination back in 1946, before the honeymoon with "our brave Russian ally" had quite faded from memory, McCarthy, at the least, cheerfully accepted support from workers under communist leadership and influence in Wisconsin's open primary. It took him almost two years to discover gold in the hills of anticommunism. In the meantime, his chief interest was in augmenting his own fortune through his relation to the real-estate lobby and certain housing interests; consider, for example, his $10,000 fee from the Lustron Corporation. He has been the demagogic opportunist, not the bigoted anticommunist fanatic. To the time of my writing, he has never employed his denunciatory power in a full-dress explanation of, and attack on, the imperialistic communism of Moscow and Peking. The objects of his wrath have been General George Marshall, former Secretary of State Dean Acheson, the British leaders Winston Churchill and Clement Attlee, and the Democratic presidential candidate, Adlai Stevenson.

---

it. But this was no moral clearance. The Department did not consider charges of the Senator's evasion of federal and state income taxes, or his campaign-funds reports which showed impecunious relatives making large gifts. These matters, the report said, lay in other hands. And technical innocence of law violation, in the Lustron case, for instance, still leaves the Senator open to charges of impropriety so grave as certainly to warrant full official investigation and possibly his expulsion from the Senate.

(Of Stevenson, McCarthy said that he might make him a "good American with a baseball bat"—or was it a slippery elm club?) He opposed the President, a member of his own party, on the choice of ambassador to Russia. For untoward events in the struggle against imperialistic communism it would appear that there is always some American or Briton to blame, always a simple formula for victory: drive the red rascals out of Washington. Thus he has become the perfect spokesman and leader for tired Americans who want to indulge their fears and hates at cheap price—at the same time to defeat communism and pay lower taxes.

In his role of Grand Inquisitor, Senator McCarthy examined James Wechsler, acknowledged ex-communist but now communism's able foe in his editorial leadership on the New York *Post*. Inquisitor McCarthy doubted Mr. Wechsler's conversion and suggested to him that some Russian commissar had told him to feign his present role the better to serve the cause. The Senator should have realized how completely that assumption might be turned against him. Certain it is that by collusion or coincidence he is following the course a philosophic communist might have chosen for him: noisy, indiscriminate criticism of communism with wholesale denunciation of secret communists in government, most of whom he cannot identify. Thus he conditions his followers for a fascist type of anticommunism, makes our Jeffersonian tradition contemptible, destroys the people's faith in their own government, and gives the communists respectability by confusing them with decent dissenters. (I have raised questions of his sixth-column service to the Kremlin in two open letters to the Senator, to which he has not replied.)

One of the worst of McCarthy's disservices to his country and to freedom is the general impression that he has created to some extent at home, and to a greater extent abroad, that his spirit controls our judicial and administrative machinery. As a matter of fact, deserving as are some of our laws and loyalty procedures of criticism and repeal or amendment, the worst feature of McCarthyism is the popular fear and suspicion which it expresses and increases. Our jails are not filled with dissenters; speech is still free to heretics who dare claim their freedom. The worst evil in America is local censorship by voluntary vigilantes in libraries and schools, and the cowardice and apathy of the public before this censorship. McCarthy is probably better rather than worse than much prejudiced or frightened and wholly unreflective public opinion.

This sobering conclusion is supported not only by his electoral success but by the responses to civil-liberties questions in a poll conducted by the National Opinion Research Center during May, 1953. Similar questions in 1946 had brought disquieting answers, but in seven years intolerance grew worse. Thus in 1953, only 45 per cent believed that the Socialist Party should be allowed to publish newspapers in this country; 15 per cent would allow *no* criticism of "government, constitution, America"; 55 per cent thought it more important "to find out all the communists in the country even if some innocent people are accused" than to protect the innocent.

This situation is in large part due to the apathy or cowardice of liberals who won't speak out. In 1951, I took part in an excellent institute on foreign policy in a Midwestern city. Local people attended the meetings but took comparatively little part in discussions. At the conclusion of the conference, I was almost timidly invited to come to an informal discussion club which would talk over the institute. I went on condition that I be taken on time to a late airplane. The informal discussion delighted me by its sense of freedom and its intelligence. But the personable young man who took me to the airport had barely seated me in his car when he said: "Now, Mr. Thomas, I hope you won't think we talk like that outside. I like my job, and the boys in the office might not like that talk." There were enough able and responsible people in that room to have changed the community climate by speaking out.

This is the sort of thing, and worse, that called forth the now famous words of Judge Learned Hand:

Risk for risk, for myself, I had rather take my chance that some traitors will escape detection than spread abroad a spirit of general suspicion and distrust, which accepts rumor and gossip in place of undismayed and unintimidated inquiry. I believe that that community is already in process of dissolution where each man begins to eye his neighbor as a possible enemy, where nonconformity with the accepted creed, political as well as religious, is a mark of disaffection; where denunciation, without specification or backing, takes the place of evidence; where orthodoxy chokes freedom of dissent; where faith in the eventual supremacy of reason has become so timid that we dare not enter our convictions in the open lists, to win or lose.

That is a description of McCarthyism, although the distinguished judge does not use that term. It is highly significant that Judge Hand is the same man who in a notable decision sustained the Smith Act, under which the communist leaders were convicted in the long trial before Judge Medina in New York. It is evident, therefore, that one can repudiate McCarthyism and still support the constitutionality of stringent anticommunist measures.

Hence it becomes necessary to examine some of those measures which, accepted by McCarthy as tools for his campaign, may also be necessary for our reasonable protection. How far are those measures consistent with the principles set forth in the preceding chapter? Is it possible to support, let us say, the Smith Act, without encouraging McCarthyism in the country at large? At what point do laws allay and at what increase the popular attitudes which Judge Hand so impressively deplored?

VII.

The Smith and McCarran Acts

FOR MANY YEARS there have been laws on the federal statute books that deal with treason, espionage, sedition, and sabotage. These laws of themselves involve no issue of civil liberty. No sane American will object to strengthening them if that seems necessary, so long as they do not transgress against the protections which the Constitution and human decency guarantee to individuals charged with grave crimes. Neither is there any well-grounded criticism of the necessity for the FBI. Its past procedures have usually been proper, and J. Edgar Hoover's voice has usually been raised for reason.

The question at issue is the point at which advocacy, either through speech or through the press, of changing government by illegal means may under the First Amendment be punished as sedition. The most important federal law dealing with this matter is the Smith Act of 1940, which makes it unlawful to conspire to advocate bringing about the forceful or violent overthrow of the government, and to organize a group so to teach. The law itself was passed in 1940, during the interval when communists and fascists were virtual allies because of the Stalin-Hitler Pact. It was avowedly directed against any communist, Nazi, or fascist fifth column in this country. But the terms of the act make no mention of foreign direction or control of organizations that might fall within the purview of the law.

For a considerable time, the law was unused. In 1941, it was first invoked against eighteen leaders of the small Trotskyist Party in Minneapolis. The actual trial occurred after the United States was at war, but the offenses alleged against the Trotskyists were committed before Pearl Harbor. It was freely charged that the federal government had been goaded into action in this case by a political obligation to the colorful and aggressive labor leader Daniel Tobin, president of the Teamsters Union, whose control in Minneapolis and perhaps outside was threatened by the strength of the Trotskyists in the Minneapolis labor movement. It is certain that the indictment of the Trotskyists was enthusiastically approved by the communists on their platforms and in their press. At that time, communist patriotism was at 212 degrees Fahrenheit, and a Trotskyist was regarded by them as the lowest form of animal life, a worse creature than the fascist devils. Nothing much was proved against the Trotskyists except that they held an extreme Marxist view of the "capitalist" war. It was not alleged that the sect was controlled by any foreign government. Probably the defendants would not have been convicted if they had not circulated some of their literature among men who had been drafted under the Selective Service Act of 1940. As it was, they were given light sentences and the case, amid the excitements of the war years, aroused comparatively little public interest. For some reason the Supreme Court refused to hear the appeal and thus avoided passing upon the constitutionality of the law.

The Department of Justice again invoked the Smith Act during the war in the mass sedition trial of alleged Nazi sympathizers, an ill-starred attempt which, as I have already recorded, was dropped after it became obvious that there was no evidence of conspiracy among these curiously assorted and mostly unadmirable defendants.

It was not until 1948 that the law was again used, this time to indict William Z. Foster and eleven other of the principal communist leaders. The judicial process moved slowly. Mr. Foster was not brought to trial because of his health. The trial of the eleven others at last got under way before Judge Medina in New York on January 17, 1949, and they were convicted ten months later, on October 14, 1949. The trial attracted nationwide attention. The conviction was fought all the way up to the Supreme Court, which in this case granted a hearing. The trial itself was generally regarded as fair, and the Supreme Court limited itself to

the question of the constitutionality of the Smith Act. Of
the eight judges who sat on the case, two, Justices Black
and Douglas, wrote dissenting opinions holding the law
unconstitutional. Justices Frankfurter and Jackson con-
curred in holding the law constitutional, but wrote separate opinions of their own in which they expressed doubt
of the wisdom of the law. Chief Justice Vinson, speaking
for himself and Justices Burton, Minton, and Reed, wrote
the prevailing opinion, which was thus the opinion of only
half the Court. This multiplicity of opinions is in itself an
illustration of the dubious conformity of the Act with the
First Amendment. Nevertheless, the Constitution is what
the Court says it is, unless and until the majority of the
Court changes its mind. The case for constitutionality had
been very ably stated by one of America's finest jurists,
Judge Learned Hand, of the circuit court, and six judges
of the Supreme Court found one reason or another to support that view. For the devotee of civil liberty, more fundamental than the question of constitutionality is the question of wisdom, and it is to that that I address myself.

Judge Hand, in the circuit court of appeals, made two
statements which I find particularly helpful in facing the
issues both of constitutionality and of wisdom, although
neither of his statements, nor both together are decisive in
support of the Smith Act. The Judge pointed out that in
law there can be no "right of revolution" of the sort to which
overeager libertarians sometimes appeal on the authority

of the Declaration of Independence. The Judge said: "The advocacy of violence may or may not fail; but in neither case can there be any 'right' to use it. Revolutions are often 'right'; but a right of revolution is a contradiction of terms. For a society which acknowledged it could not stop at tolerating conspiracies to overthrow it but must include their execution."

Judge Hand also laid down a rule for interpreting clear and present danger: "In each case, [the courts] must ask whether the gravity of the 'evil,' discounted by its probability, justifies such evasion of free speech as is necessary to avoid the danger." Justice Frankfurter in his separate opinion upholding the constitutionality of the Smith Act referred to Judge Hand's rule as only "a sonorous formula . . . a euphemistic disguise for an unresolved conflict." The fault lies, I think, not with Judge Hand's formula but with the great difficulty in making a judgment which has to be related to present circumstances as well as to general principles. I prefer Judge Hand's formula to Justice Frankfurter's apparent willingness to let Congress decide what speech is perilous and write the decision into rigid law.

I follow the admirable analysis of the Supreme Court decision published by the American Civil Liberties Union in believing that the Smith Act as interpreted by the majority of the Court may now be applied: "(1) To prohibit a number of persons (but not an individual), (2) from advocating (but not discussing), (3) under certain circumstances (but not under all circumstances), (4) violent overthrow of the government (but not necessarily any other end)."

It must be remembered that the verdict of the jury found these leaders of the Communist Party guilty only, as Justice Black put it, of agreeing "to assemble and to talk and publish certain ideas at a future date; the indictment is that they conspired to organize the Communist Party and to use newspapers or other publications in the future to teach and advocate forcible overthrow of the government." The trial itself brought out facts about the nature of the Communist Party of the kind I have already set forth, but those facts have never included overt acts of sedition in the United States. (It was a group of select individuals who practiced espionage, not the Party as a whole.) The question of clear and present danger was all-important. On that issue, Judge Medina ruled. He did not allow the jury to pass on it. The constitutionality of his ruling was upheld by the higher courts. It seems evident to me that clear and present danger should be regarded as a matter of fact, on which the jury should be allowed to pass as on other facts.

It is impossible for anyone in these times to be absolutely certain of the imminence of the danger presented by a conspiratorial party which in action has proved itself part of an international movement of the nature of communism. There is no reasonable doubt that the Party believes and teaches that its followers must be ready to use violence at some time in its service. But I think the imminence of such violence, on the evidence offered in the various trials that have now been held under the Smith Act, is exceedingly dubious. And the opportunity to deal with this theory of violence through open discussion is very great.

On the other hand, in the light of events, what Judge Hand in his formula calls "the evasion of free speech" is a growing evil in the United States. We have no statistical device for measuring the precise extent to which the Smith Act as now enforced has contributed to a general atmosphere of fear and suspicion and has encouraged activities on a local level for interfering with freedom of speech. Public opinion, and sometimes the police, do not easily follow the limitations set forth by the Supreme Court on the right to interfere with free speech in the name of national security. There is small doubt that the Smith Act and the recurring trials under it have contributed directly to the situation in America which Justice Hand himself, in the passage previously quoted, so eloquently deplored.

One event in particular would seem to support this contention. A professor of philosophy, W. Lou Tandy, at the State Teachers College, Emporia, Kansas, was one of 250 signers of an amnesty petition in the form of an open letter to ex-President Truman asking him to grant amnesty to the eleven leaders of the Communist Party first convicted under the Smith Act, a petition which Mr. Truman denied. When the names of the petitioners, many of them outstanding Americans, became public, the authorities of the college asked for Dr. Tandy's resignation. When the professor refused it, the regents of the college, apparently on the advice of the acting president, voted for his dismissal, on the ground that Dr. Tandy, by seeking mercy for communists, had affiliated himself with communists to the hurt of the school—this, although the right of petition, guaranteed by the Constitution, had been exercised merely to seek mercy for men convicted under a law the constitutionality or wisdom of which had been doubted by half the Supreme Court.

That law, as I have previously pointed out, is being used by the government to arrest successive waves of leaders of the still-legal Communist Party, thus making it almost impossible for the Party to carry on open activity. This is, in effect, outlawry of the Party—despite the insistence of prosecutors and judges that the Party itself is not on trial. Judge Dimmock in a second trial of leaders in New York did, to be sure, discharge two of them on the ground that the evidence did not sufficiently connect them with the illegal conspiratorial activities of the other leaders. But it is not a distinction, given the nature of the Communist Party, which the layman can easily follow. It is a practical certainty that all communist leaders will be obliged to follow the universal custom of communists throughout the world with respect to their theories of force and violence. No matter what prudential denials communists may make, we may assume it will not be difficult, especially in the temper of our times, for the government to get convictions. Indeed, by September 1, 1953 it already had got eighty indictments in various parts of the country, made sixty-four arrests, and obtained fifty-six convictions. The theory that a party can be legal when so many of its leaders are guilty is very thin.

If the purpose of these convictions is to strengthen the actual security of the United States, the government's success is dubious. I doubt if the United States is safer against enemies within and without because Eugene Dennis, Elizabeth Gurley Flynn, and their companions are in jail. It is obvious that the convictions have not strengthened a popular sense of security. Rather they have tended to augment an indiscriminate fear and suspicion which vents itself in demands for victims and yet more victims. About the best that can be said for the trials, especially the first trial before Judge Medina, is that they have established, under rules of evidence, many important facts about the nature of organized communism. Those facts, however, were available years ago at a lower price to our country and its ideals.

This low opinion of the usefulness of the Smith Act in protecting American security finds somewhat unexpected confirmation in Attorney General Brownell's statements in an interview published by *U.S. News and World Report* (September 4, 1953). The Attorney General began by saying that the FBI thinks the Communist Party "a greater menace now than at any time." Asked why, he replied, "The Communists have gone underground since the Smith trials started. They are better organized and detection is more difficult."

I question the FBI's estimate of the magnitude of the internal communist danger, because the tides of public opinion now run so strongly against communism. But unquestionably detection is more difficult. In view of that admission, the Attorney General's later rather perfunctory statement that the Smith Act "is an excellent law and has done a great deal, first, to stop the activities of the top communists, and, second, to make the American people realize the danger of what they are facing from communist activities in this country" does not have much weight. We didn't need the Smith Act convictions to educate us.

When the Smith Act was before Congress back in 1940, I thought it wholly unnecessary in the struggle against sedition and urged President Roosevelt to oppose and, if necessary, veto the law. I then thought that it would be enough to strengthen existing laws, already on the statute books, dealing with overt acts. In the present state of public opinion, if not of the law, I should regard it as sounder and wiser tactics for Congress to substitute a better law for the Smith Act than simply to repeal it. A comprehensive law on sedition might have some value even if it should deal with what may already be crimes under the common law or previous statutes. I shall state in layman's language three types of offenses which might properly be punished:

1. Teaching, by an individual or a group, of methods of espionage or of sabotage of security operations.

2. The advocacy or actual formation of a private, secret or semisecret military body. William Z. Foster, in his *Toward a Soviet America,* a book written before communists felt the necessity of masking their plans so carefully, declared categorically: "Even before the seizure of power, the workers will organize the Red Guard. . . . The leader of the revolution in all its stages is the Communist Party." I should like this part of the new law so framed that it would apply to any revival of Ku Klux Klan masked bands which engage in their own types of violence and often usurp the functions of police.

3. Advocacy by an individual, or a conspiratorial group, of specific illegal acts of force and violence immediately directed to the overthrow of government on any level. For example, advocacy of a specific armed demonstration before a city hall at a definite time. Such advocacy is, of course, a very different thing from a general advocacy of possible force and violence in some indefinite future. It has to do with acts which there is not time to prevent by public discussion or simply by turning light on them. The law should provide that in all such cases the jury should be allowed to pass on the facts indicating concrete and imminent danger.

It is this last section of the law that might be most liable to abuse, but the record both of communism and fascism on the world stage argues that there may be need for it. It is never possible completely to guard any law against abuse. For that we have to depend upon the vigilance of intelligent public opinion, and in America today it would be easier to educate public opinion in proper vigilance if it were marshalled in support of a law that is as adequate as that which I suggest. None of the cases so far brought by the government against the communist leaders would properly fall under any provision of the law that I have outlined.

The second law which the federal government is in the process of using against communists is the McCarran Internal Security Act. This law is a strange mish-mash. As passed over the President's veto on September 23, 1950, it contained provisions strengthening the sedition laws, forbidding picketing of federal courts, imposing onerous requirements on aliens, setting up machinery for the internment of communist suspects in the event of war, and providing elaborately for the registration of communist-action and communist-front organizations and the individuals in them.

The provision against picketing federal courts is sound. Such picketing is or may be a form of intimidation of jurors or potential jurors. The provisions concerning aliens have been inserted with some modifications for the better in the more recent McCarran-Walter Act, which will be discussed in a later chapter.

The provisions giving the President power to order the internment in time of war, invasion, or insurrection in aid of a foreign enemy of those concerning whom "there is reasonable ground to believe" that they will be guilty of espionage or sedition in some form, have probably as many qualifications and protections of the individual as one could hope for in time of serious crisis. The internees are not to be subjected to forced labor. No one is to be interned without a hearing, and some appeal to the courts is to be allowed. In days gone by, I knew of communists who looked forward rather cheerfully to internment in a spot relatively remote from atomic bombing, a place in comparative safety, from which they could emerge for prospective rule amid the ruins of war. Nevertheless, the adoption of any provisions for any sort of internment camps at this particular juncture, with so limited discussion as attended this particular feature of the McCarran Act, did far more to create apprehension here and abroad concerning American poise and American appreciation of liberty than to establish confidence among our people for their future security.

The fact that these provisions were in the bill at all is a commentary on the ineptness of liberals in both the Eighty-first and Eighty-second Congresses, in which the Democratic Party nominally had a majority. United action by the liberals, vigorous debate, and greater use of ridicule against the bill would, I am certain, have developed enough opposition to sustain the President's powerful veto of it. The weakness of liberals in fighting this bill was matched by their failure at a later date to sustain the President's veto of the McCarran-Walter Act and is of itself a commentary on our time.

What happened was this: Senator Karl Mundt and Richard Nixon, then a congressman, had been pushing the Mundt-Nixon Bill, nominally dedicated to the pious end of dealing with communism by turning light on it, but actually imposing clumsy and fantastic restrictions on freedom. Senator Pat McCarran, of Nevada, was then chairman of the Judiciary Committee in the nominally Democratic Senate. He adopted the Mundt-Nixon Bill with minor changes and added a good deal to it. The liberals, terrified by the Hiss case and its repercussions, instead of fighting the Mundt-Nixon Bill head on, had the bright idea of introducing something which they said was better, namely the Kilgore Bill, setting up internment camps in the event of war. Senator McCarran at first cried out with horror against this bill as a violation of the constitutional rights of Americans. Liberals brought similar charges against his pet bill. So they compromised by incorporating the best, or worst, features of both measures in the McCarran Act.

The registration features are now the most important. They are only just coming into operation, and the law of itself provides such endless opportunities for legal appeals that it may yet serve as a PWA measure for otherwise unemployed lawyers. Briefly the situation is this: Both communist-action groups (the Communist Party, its subdivisions, and its direct agencies) and communist-front or

communist-dominated organizations are supposed to go
through a certain machinery of registry, not only of their
officers but of their members. They were given a certain
length of time to register voluntarily. No organization registered, since to do so would have involved it in an impossible burden of reporting and would have subjected its
members to various disabilities, such as denial of passport
and any right at all to any sort of federal employment.

When the time limit for voluntary registration had
expired, the Attorney General under the law certified the
Communist Party, and later certain alleged front organizations, to a five-man subversive control board set up under
the law. This board held solemn and properly conducted
hearings concerning the Communist Party and then certified, correctly under the terms of the law, that it should
now be compelled to register. Like proceedings are going
on involving various front organizations, all of which will
have a right to appeal.

After this long process is exhausted, organizations refusing to register will be subject to heavy fines and their
individual officers to fines and imprisonment. The members
of the organizations will then be compulsorily registered
and subjected to the penalties which they might have as-
sumed voluntarily. It appears, however, that all these penalties may be avoided if at the last minute, after all appeals
are exhausted but before compulsory registration, the organization is dissolved. There is nothing to prevent its practical reappearance with a different name and different offi-

cers a few days later, when the process could start over
again.

In effect, the law is a clumsy and expensive indirect
way of outlawing the Communist Party and various of its
fronts. The law's appeal for voluntary registration is a good
deal like asking a society of prospective but unconvicted
burglars to step up and leave names and addresses of members with the sheriff, who will then expect them to report
to him weekly. (To make the parallel more complete one
must imagine that the association of prospective burglars
had given a general indication of the region in which they
would operate.)

This sort of thing is nonsense. It makes American law
ridiculous in the eyes of foreign observers and tends to increase, not to allay, the unhealthy atmosphere of suspicion
here at home. It is very doubtful if the McCarran Act will
ever do anything to the communists as individuals or as a
party except to give them a chance for relatively cheap
martyrdom by refusing to register. The slow working of
the law will have given them plenty of time to plan for
underground or evasive action. Innocent members of alleged front organizations will be the chief victims.

VIII.

Legislative Investigations and Individual Rights

SOON AFTER the Republicans took office, their legislative inquiries by (1) the Permanent Committee to Investigate the Executive Departments, of which Senator Joseph McCarthy is chairman, (2) the subcommittee of the Judiciary Committee, of which William E. Jenner is chairman, and (3) the House Committee on Un-American Activities, of which Harold H. Velde is chairman, became centers of widespread controversy.

These committees, by reason of the personal qualifications or disqualifications of their chairmen, their methods of investigation, and the range or threatened range of their inquiries, have stirred up not only fear of dissent but also strong criticism by church and civic bodies, educational associations, and newspapers. (The Jenner Committee has,

however, thus far proceeded with an unexpected degree
of propriety in the *manner* of its investigations, if not in its
objectivity.)

Some regional organizations of the American Legion
in Nebraska, Oregon, and New York are vehemently opposed to federal investigations of schools, a heartening fact
considering the tendency of the Legion to identify patriotism with uncritical conformity. The average congressman,
however, was apparently convinced that public opinion
supported these inquisitorial inquiries, so that he voted
appropriations for them with little or no criticism of their
methods. (Some congressional criticism came later.)

Among liberals, criticism of these committees was
sometimes carried to the length of demanding their total
abolition or, more usually, some sort of limitation on the
range of their inquiry by action in the federal courts. Such
extreme positions are scarcely justified. In the more than
160 years of our constitutional history, Congress has, on
the whole, served the public interest well by legislative inquiry. Under our system of government, the executive is
not, as in a parliamentary country, itself a kind of committee of the legislative body. It is an independent branch
of government. Congress does not receive from it, as a
matter of course, drafts of bills. Congress is dependent on
its own activity to check on executive recommendations
and performances and to guide its legislation. In our various wars, these legislative committees have served a real
use in discovering and checking waste and corruption. The

work of Senate committees or subcommittees such as the Walsh Committee, which brought the Teapot Dome oil scandal to light, and the LaFollette Committee, which made a notable report on civil liberties, will live in American history.

It is true that legislative committees can abuse their proper functions and set themselves up as inquisitors into the beliefs and conduct of private citizens to a degree far out of line with the proper check on government operations or the framing of wise legislation. But I doubt if an absolute legal formula can safely be framed to distinguish between legitimate legislative inquiry into the *acts* of a man or group of men and illegitimate inquiry into *opinions* and *beliefs* which explain and inspire their acts. What is clearly wrong, if not illegal, is a legislative committee's random exploration of the field of opinion or of the fields of religion and education. In such fields any legitimate inquiry should have specific relation to legitimate action by Congress or a state legislature. It is conceivable that a committee in the McCarthyist spirit may sometime so outrageously exceed its legitimate range of inquiry as to bring upon itself limitation by judicial action. But that would be an extreme and probably a dangerous remedy.

The legitimate range of inquiry for legislative committees, under the most recent ruling of the Supreme Court, is great. It is not a wholesome situation when legislators have to be regulated by courts rather than by sound democratic public opinion. Courts are by no means infallible.

Some of the liberals who now cry out for legal action would have cried with at least equal vehemence against an appeal to the courts in the early days of the New Deal, when the "nine old men" of the Supreme Court constituted, in liberal thought, a major block to progress. It must be admitted that the techniques of some useful legislative committees during years of great New Deal activity were not too scrupulous in protecting all the rights and dignities of citizens brought before them.

It is, of course, open to individuals in particular cases to appeal to courts against specific abuses of constitutional rights of which they consider themselves victims. Under our laws, no committee can directly punish a refractory witness. The House or the Senate must vote in favor of contempt proceedings, which must be brought before a court. It is not the constitutional or the legal practice of congressional inquiry which requires amendment, so much as the spirit and judgment with which the investigatory process is used, and here our appeal in the final analysis must be directed to the court of public opinion.

We shall be better able to judge current congressional inquiries and their effect on the rights of citizens if we examine history, beginning with the constitution by the House of a special committee on un-American activities. This committee was first set up in 1938, on motion of Martin Dies, Democrat, of Texas, who became its first chairman. It became a regular committee of the House and so continued until 1949. Dies and his successors, John Rankin, Demo-

crat, of Mississippi, and J. Parnell Thomas, Republican, of
New Jersey, were far removed in character from ideal ex-
plorers of a field so vaguely and subjectively defined as that
of "un-American activities." Until the Hiss case they exposed no dangerous underground activities. Mostly they
noisily compiled lists of real and alleged fellow travelers.
Their techniques of inquiry were even more arbitrary and
more unfair to individuals than those in use today. For these
and more personal reasons—for instance, Rankin's racial
prejudice and Thomas' lack of honor—Jefferson and Lincoln would have regarded these inquisitors as outrageous
arbiters of true Americanism.

In the years when Martin Dies and John Rankin were
chief inquisitors, America presented a curious ambivalence.
The House of Representatives always felt compelled by
public opinion to support the committee of inquiry. Nevertheless, it was so widely discredited that it was frequently
referred to as the Un-American Committee. Presidents
Roosevelt and Truman felt safe in ignoring the successive
Democratic chairmen of this legislative inquisition but not
in repudiating the committee. There came a day in 1945
when even in Texas Martin Dies found his fame something
of a handicap, so that he retired from politics. By 1952, he
felt that he and his brain child were sufficiently rehabili-
tated again to aspire to Congress. He was easily elected.
But he was not again put on the committee to which once
he had given his name. By this time, the House Committee
had acquired standing and respect by its work in bringing

to light the facts which led to the indictment of Alger Hiss
and to the definite revelation of espionage practiced by certain government employees in favor of the Kremlin. Not
even men as critical as I of the old House Committee could
challenge its procedures in uncovering the Hiss case. Its
work under Chairman Velde is not of that order of importance, and it has been reckless in releasing charges in advance of any opportunity to reply.

Prior to the sensational charges made by Whittaker
Chambers against Alger Hiss, enough testimony had come
to light to make it impossible to allege that there was no
need for any sort of official inquiry into acts of disloyalty
and subversion, the proper legal remedies for them, and
punishments of them. The FBI was properly prohibited by
law from conducting such inquiry on its own authority or
from giving publicity to the results of the inquiries it made
in pursuance of its duties. The unsatisfactory record of the
House Committee under Dies, Rankin, and Thomas was
such that some other investigatory agency was preferable
—an agency lifted, as far as possible, above partisan politics, whose findings would not be a football, kicked about
by rival candidates to Congress.

Canada had seemed to pave the way to an effective
procedure in line with proper respect for civil liberty by
setting up a Royal Commission of Inquiry, composed of distinguished citizens, which studied the problem presented
by the help Canadians had given to Russian spies in Canada during World War II. Its published report is a model

of proper and useful reporting. A number of Americans, including myself, independently arrived at the conclusion, before the indictment of Alger Hiss, that Congress should set up a somewhat similar committee of distinguished American citizens, to be appointed by the President in collaboration with Congress, to study and report on the facts and the changes of law or administrative procedure which might be necessary to strengthen the country against the harm that could be brought upon it by disloyal and untrustworthy civil servants.

Such proposals got little or no attention from Congress. Instead the Senate set out to rival the House. It gave us the two widely roving investigatory committees we have today: the one, a standing committee on government operations, and the other, a subcommittee of the Judiciary Committee.

Not even Senator McCarthy's great influence has been sufficient to prevent considerable rivalry between congressional committees. The situation has been further complicated by the fact that McCarthy considers he has a commission to investigate a little of everything, even matters specifically within the competence of other Senate committees or subcommittees. Thus, he took a flier at investigating the Voice of America and the State Department Information Service in general, a matter to be referred to later, although there was a subcommittee of the Senate Foreign Relations Committee of the Eighty-third Congress, whose chairman was Senator Hickenlooper, of Iowa, specif-

ically directed to the duty of inquiring into these important matters. In this case, a little senatorial competition was
good for the cause of truth. The Hickenlooper subcommittee gave the Voice of America its first chance to reply to
sensational charges to which the McCarthy Committee
had given great publicity, and it ultimately issued a sober
and responsible report.

So much for the history behind the activities of the
congressional committees which have raised serious problems for civil liberties by the degree to which they have
pressed inquiry into the personal opinions and beliefs of
free American citizens. To a very considerable extent, the
whole issue has been further complicated by the extent
to which it has been involved in partisan politics. Despite
the fact that President Truman on his own initiative set up
a drastic procedure of loyalty tests, it pleased the Republicans to hold him and the Democratic Party responsible, at
least by carelessness, for a dangerous communist interpenetration in the government. There *was* such interpenetration, unduly minimized by liberals and more unduly exaggerated by prominent Republicans. Mr. Truman's offhand remark that the Hiss case was a red herring had very
unfortunate results and gave partisan orators a major talking point.

Present criticism of our congressional inquisitors falls
under three heads: (1) the subject matter of their investigations, (2) the technical procedures of investigation which
allegedly encroach on the citizen's rights, and (3) the

efforts of committees, or rather their chairmen, to manipulate publicity to catch headlines and to gain personal or
partisan advantage.

The most vehement critic of the McCarthy, Jenner,
and Velde committees can scarcely claim that their investigations have as yet passed the border line into prov-
inces legally beyond their power. Legislators have a right
to investigate disloyalty where they think it may be found.
In terms of sound public policy—as distinct from mere
legality—the House Committee on Un-American Activities has been the worst offender. Chairman Velde has shown
a considerable desire to conduct a fishing expedition into
loyalty in the churches, from which he has been partially
restrained by others on his committee. One of them, however, Congressman Jackson of California, was especially
anxious to examine Bishop Oxnam, of the Methodist
Church. The latter in an open hearing rendered so good an
account of himself in defense of civil liberty that he seemed
to clear the air. Nevertheless, a few weeks later, on September 11, 1953, the Committee released testimony given in
closed hearings by former communists Joseph Zack Kornfeder, Benjamin Gitlow, and Manning Johnson, reporting
substantial communist success in boring from within Protestant churches and Jewish religious organizations. Mr.
Kornfeder placed the number of clergymen who are secret
members of the Communist Party at six hundred while two
thousand more, he said, were pretty "close to the machine."
He placed from three thousand to four thousand "among

the fellow-travelling category." A number of more or less prominent clergymen were specifically named, notably by the bitter Benjamin Gitlow.

The Jenner Committee—not to be outdone—at the same time released far less specific testimony about two men allegedly "active participants in an effort to establish a communist cell in Catholic organizations."

My own experience in the last thirty years and my general knowledge of communist tactics would lead me to believe that there were and are persistent communist attempts at interpenetration in the churches. I should credit those attempts with some success. I have known a handful of clergymen and rabbis who may not have paid regular dues to the Communist Party but who gave every indication of complete loyalty to the communist line. I have known, or known of, many more whose continuing sympathy with communism did little credit to their understanding of the basic conflict between their own religious philosophy and the philosophy of communism. They could not, however, fairly be classified as communists, and the communist causes or fronts which they and occasionally other clergymen supported had an ethical appeal.

However, I know enough about the ex-communist witnesses, as well as some of the persons they mentioned, to believe that the extent and depth of communist interpenetration was grossly exaggerated in the testimony that the Velde Committee released before giving its victims opportunity to reply. By no means does it follow that all or most of the 2300 clergymen reported in 1953 by the *Daily Worker* as signing petitions for clemency for the convicted spies Ethel and Julius Rosenberg were therefore communist sympathizers, as Mr. Kornfeder alleged in his testimony. And it is fantastically slanderous for any ex-communist to denounce such men as John Haynes Holmes and the late Rabbi Judah Magnes as communist stooges.

On the same date that the Velde Committee released its testimony concerning communist-controlled clergymen, it released testimony by the popular actress Lucille Ball concerning her past connections with communism. I should judge that at one time she was, on her own statement, closer to the Party than most of the clergymen under criticism. But everybody loves Lucy, and very properly that suspicious investigator Congressman Jackson, of the Committee, emphasized the fact that there is no evidence that Miss Ball ever joined the Communist Party or that she has had any connection with it in recent years. There should not be one standard of procedure for reporting on a popular actress and another for clergymen.

Certainly there is no prima facie evidence of such communist interpenetration in the churches as to justify political intervention to punish or discredit the churches or their clergy.

Chairman McCarthy of the Senate Committee came close to the line of illegal and certainly unjust interference with the press in his examination of his strong critic James Wechsler, editor of the New York *Post*. Legally, Chairman

McCarthy probably saved himself by alleging that he was inquiring into the opinions of Wechsler the author of a book or books in some of the United States Information Libraries abroad, rather than into the opinions of James Wechsler the editorial critic of McCarthyism. Very little was said about the book or books—they weren't even properly identified. The examination was highly personal. That it did not have a greater effect in intimidating the press was not McCarthy's fault.

Mr. Wechsler persuaded the American Society of Newspaper Editors to appoint a committee to consider whether McCarthy's treatment of him threatened freedom of the press. Unfortunately the committee of eleven could not agree. The committee chairman, J. R. Wiggins, managing editor of the Washington *Post,* and three others signed a statement to the effect that McCarthy's methods were not only a threat to freedom of the press but also "a peril to American freedom." Senator McCarthy retaliated by threatening to investigate the Washington *Post* and its managing editor, alleging that the independence of the press was menaced by the subsidies implicit in the postal rates for newspapers—which, by the way, Mr. Wiggins does not support. This counterattack was characteristic of the Senator. For instance, when *Time* displeased him he wrote to advertisers in it asking them to boycott the magazine. (One would like to say that this flagrant attack on free speech and a free press by economic pressure is peculiar to McCarthy. It is, alas, a method employed with in-

creasing boldness by religious, racial, nationalist, and other
special-interest groups. It is one of the more alarming ex-
amples of McCarthyism in action.)

The greatest amount of discussion has attended congressional inquiries into communist influence in schools,
colleges, and universities. Mr. Robert Morris, chief counsel
for the Jenner Committee and previously for the same committee under McCarran, has observed fairer standards of
procedure than many other committees have used. Under
his direction, the Committee has not gone off into a general
fishing expedition; it has not indiscriminately blackened
the name of dissenters.

In a somewhat different setting than prevails today,
with a different public frame of mind, it might well be
argued that the congressional committees have been allay-
ing a general and unjust suspicion of teachers by directing
inquiry to a comparatively few specific cases. Official investigation cannot be dismissed as altogether unimportant
to a nation which is entitled to the facts about communism
in schools and colleges. President Harry D. Gideonse of
Brooklyn College, for example, welcomed the Jenner Committee's investigation in his struggle against communism.

Nevertheless, the preponderance of evidence indicates
that the Jenner Committee, like McCarthy's own and the
Velde Committee, is now doing more harm than good. It
seems to threaten an unwarranted degree of federal interference with privately supported schools and colleges, and

with public schools directly under the control of the different states. These inquiries tend to promote a degree of fear
and perturbation on college campuses and schools which
is more widely hurtful to freedom of thought and excellence
of teaching than current communist activities.

The harm done cannot be measured in statistics of
teachers dismissed. The latter are, as I write, comparatively
few in number, and the usual reason for their dismissal is
their refusal to answer legitimate questions put to them.
This matter is of such importance that I shall quote rather
extensively from Robert M. Hallett's admirable summary
of the Jenner and Velde Committees' "teacher probes,"
published in the *Christian Science Monitor,* July 21, 1953.

> There were 146 witnesses before both committees
> whose testimony in major part pertained to education.
> Of these, 74 teachers, professors, and students declined
> to answer at least some of the questions put to them by
> the committees. The others were cooperative witnesses,
> or persons no longer teaching or nonacademic members
> of university staffs.
>
> Of the 74 who declined to answer the committees'
> questions, 30 were dismissed; dismissal action has been
> started against two; eight have resigned; 12 cases still
> are pending; five have been suspended; 10 retained; two
> Harvard University students were not expelled, and the
> case of a Chicago University student is still under study.
>
> In addition, four teachers fell into special categories.
> A University of Buffalo professor lost his tenure as an
> associate professor but was retained on a year-to-year
> basis. A Columbia University professor came under the

ruling of trustees limiting the number of annual appointments; her appointment was not renewed—the university said the decision had nothing to do with her testimony. A Laguna Beach, Calif., school official was dismissed as principal but offered a position as elementary grade teacher. Another teacher at Los Angeles State College who had been on a year-to-year basis had been notified prior to the committee hearings that he no longer was needed.

A breakdown category of 42 university professors who declined to testify yields the following:

5 retained.

3 resigned.

1 lost tenure but still employed.

5 suspended.

12 cases pending.

14 dismissed.

1 annual appointment not renewed.

1 annual employee notified no longer needed.

For the 29 elementary and secondary school teachers the figures show:

5 retained.

4 resigned.

1 suspended.

16 dismissed.

2 dismissal action begun.

1 dismissed as principal but kept as teacher.

Of the five retained in the last category three were employed by schools which committees indicated were Communist-controlled and no punitive action might be expected.

Of the other 72 witnesses before both committees who are outside the category of present teachers who refused to testify, 28 were former teachers who declined to answer; 35 (not all teachers) cooperated with the committees to varying degrees, and 9 declined to testify who were in nonteaching jobs on or off school grounds.

Of the 35 cooperative witnesses, 15 were teachers who admitted Communist membership or sympathies in the past but denied it today; 6 were eminent educators or school administrators completely unconnected with communism and called to testify about conditions in their schools. . . .

It is probable that the Jenner and Velde committees will continue their work as a result of which educational authorities may discharge more teachers and possibly some students.

It should be observed that while a student may technically be subject to disciplinary action for resorting to the Fifth Amendment to avoid answering questions on his communist connections, the student's failure to answer involves far less potential danger than the teacher's. The communist student, unlike the communist teacher, does not hold a sensitive position. He should be entitled to study, just as he should be entitled to earn his living. The educational process over and over has changed wrongheaded, youthful ideas which are more likely to be confirmed by martyrdom.

Whatever one thinks of the foregoing facts, the greatest harm done by the Jenner and Velde committees in the field of education is indirect; federal investigation has tended to incite or augment community suspicion. The situation was thus described in an American survey by that able paper *The Economist* of London, by a correspondent writing from the United States. He said: "The damage has long since been done. It is to be measured, if such measurements are possible, in terms of opinions left unexpressed out of timidity, letters to the editor left unposted, lectures toned down for respectability's sake, memberships in liberal organizations abandoned. It is shown in an ever increasing tendency to look before one leaps—and then, perhaps, not to leap at all."

This judgment is confirmed on the public-school level by the research division of the National Education Association, which reported to the NEA convention at the end of June, 1953, that there was a tendency for school superintendents to discourage discussion of controversial topics because of fear of community reactions. These issues were considered most controversial: religious education, sex education, communism, socialized medicine, local politics, race relations, UNESCO, and the United Nations. Quite a comprehensive list.

At the college level, *Time* (April 15, 1953) in its section on Education, quoted remarks, opinions, or experiences of professors and instructors from ten widely scattered university campuses, which it grouped under the head "Danger Signals." They fully confirm the opinion expressed in *The Economist*. *Time* remarks: "The academic motto for 1953 is fast becoming: Don't say, don't write, don't go."

On the record there is still much freedom of speech for dissenters in our colleges if they have courage to use it. But the fear engendered by congressional investigations is dangerous in its effect on a somewhat timorous profession.

In the matter of *procedure* in inquiry, too many congressional committees have sinned grievously against fair play to individuals. But even the critical ACLU agrees that in this respect the current committees have employed, as a rule, fairer procedures than some of their predecessors. The old Dies Committee was a peculiarly great sinner. Congress is slowly developing a little conscience in the matter, and there are, as I write, two bills before the Senate, introduced by Senators Morse and Kefauver respectively, and two in the House, introduced by Representatives Keating and Javits respectively, which would set up codes of greater or less value. In June, 1953, the House Rules Committee set up a subcommittee to study the whole matter.

The need for procedural reform is evident. Many a man has awaked in the morning to find himself suddenly stigmatized by some congressional hearing. He has waited for days for a chance to reply. He has not been allowed to confront hostile witnesses or been informed adequately of the information against him. In hundreds of cases he has never been heard at all. Lists of suspect individuals and agencies running into the thousands were thus compiled and publicized by federal and state committees with no redress for individuals named in them. Opportunities for hearings came later if at all. The famous Attorney General's

list in constant use in loyalty or security proceedings was
made up in like fashion and made public without hearings.
Opportunities for hearings on it came later, if at all. (Attorney General Brownell has announced his willingness to
give hearings to complaining organizations. But in many
cases this is a hearing after punishment—that is, listing.)
In recent hearings, McCarthy was grossly unfair to the
Voice of America and certain of its employees because he
gave so much opportunity to critics and so little opportunity—and so late—for the victims to reply. His has been a
hit-and-run method of inquiry to the accompaniment of a
brass band. It is reasonable to suppose that he could have
discovered more by quieter tactics.

In my more optimistic mood I hope that the paralyzing
effects of McCarthyist investigations upon so many citizens
and teachers will be offset by the increased attention which
teachers themselves are paying to the true meaning of academic freedom, an attention which has found expression
in some eloquent and thoughtful statements by individuals
and by educational bodies. But courage has not sifted down
to rank-and-file teachers and students. They prefer to divert suspicion of disloyalty by practicing the conformity
dear to the heart of totalitarians.

The sharpest controversy in this field at present concerns the proper line of conduct for witnesses to take. Do
they defend civil liberty by refusing to answer questions
bearing upon their own political beliefs and connections?
Is there a sacred right of silence in this field, which not only

can but should be protected by an appeal to the Fifth Amendment which offers sanctuary against self-incrimination? What should be the treatment of those who refuse to answer?

In the Blau case in 1950, the Supreme Court ruled that an individual might not be compelled to answer questions regarding his Communist Party activities, if he should plead the right to avoid self-incrimination, because, conceivably, under the Smith Act his answers might tend to furnish "a link in the chain of evidence" leading to prosecution. Others have since rushed for protection to this precarious sanctuary. While it may protect them from further inquiry or criminal proceedings, it does not, as we have seen, protect their jobs.

My own very strong conviction is that civil liberty will never be served in these inquiries by making a fetish of the right to silence. That right has little relation to the right of secret ballot in an election. In the social value of such secrecy we all believe. Dr. Hu Shih, the Chinese scholar and former ambassador, may have suggested a nearer parallel to the resort to the Fifth Amendment by his poignant reference to the cruel denial of "the right to silence" in Red China. Thus he explained the fact that his own son in China was compelled to denounce his father and all his works. (Dr. Hu Shih later told me that he was glad his son had thus denounced him. It would make it easier for his other friends to do the same thing and thus save their lives and some degree of liberty. They knew that he did not believe they meant those words.) This denial of the right to silence in communist or fascist countries is really a compulsion to false speech. Heroes will resist it.

College professors don't become heroes by a dubious legal dodge to escape answering legitimate questions, pertinent to an inquiry. The men who have given reality to the rights of conscience and freedom of speech never have won their victories by anticipating the contention that the highest right of free citizens holding responsible positions in our democracy is to silence concerning their opinions about, and their relations to, great movements which involve the freedom of us all.

I find myself surprised that some communist or apologist for communism, knowing the hurt to himself that must attend his refusal to answer questions, does not choose to speak up and use, as he well might, the Velde or the Jenner Committee as a sounding board for himself and his cause. Instead, if any communist teacher has been examined he has preferred to evade the issue on plea of the right of silence, a plea that others, who may not be communists, have also offered.

Many of those who have invoked the Fifth Amendment, or their friends in their behalf, have insisted that it was unfair to regard their act as a confession of past Communist Party membership or close association with the movement. They are right that in a criminal trial such refusal to testify must not be counted against the defendant. But in the setting of a legislative inquiry which is not a criminal trial, the refusal to answer necessarily awakens in the public mind a strong suspicion, if not conviction, of guilt. There is no valid evidence that a noncommunist would incriminate himself by telling the truth about himself and his past.

To this argument, two answers are sometimes given. The first, a lawyer explains, was given him by a client, who claimed that if he had truthfully denied connection with communism, he would, he feared, have been indicted on framed evidence for perjury. The lawyer himself did not seem to believe that his client's fears had weight. It is still a very difficult thing, even on good evidence, to get a conviction on perjury before an American jury. And a man who refuses to speak up for the truth because of such a fear is a coward rather than a champion of freedom. The public has a right to expect candor of its servants, emphatically including those who, as teachers, should inspire our youth in search of truth. Judge Youngdahl's rulings on various counts in the indictment of Owen Lattimore for perjury illustrate the care that courts will give in such cases to the rights of individuals.

The second justification for refusal to answer a question on communist connections is the allegation that if the witness should answer in the affirmative but deny present connection with the Party, he would next be asked to name his associates in the days when he was connected with it. That kind of information all of us hate to give. Dislike of tattletales or informers is ingrained in us from childhood.

A few witnesses have dealt with the question by acknowledging their former connections with the Communist Party but refusing to give the names of their associates on the grounds that none of those associates gave any sign of being guilty of disloyal acts today, that doubtless some of them had changed their minds, and they should not be subjected to unnecessary inquisition.

The law can hardly admit the legal justification of this exercise of individual judgment concerning the information to be given or withheld from authorities responsible for the peace and security of the country. Nevertheless, it would be very well for investigating committees to respect the reluctance of witnesses and to refrain from citing them for contempt for refusal to answer unless very grave dangers to our peace and safety may be involved. As a matter of fact, there have been several cases in which no contempt proceedings have been lodged against witnesses who assured committees of their willingness to answer questions about their own beliefs and connections, past or present, but not questions about the beliefs and connections of former friends.*

After the first draft of this chapter was written, that very great scientist and noble humanitarian Professor Albert Einstein earnestly championed not the right but the duty of "intellectuals" to refuse to answer questions concerning their political beliefs in congressional inquiries,

---

* *Commentary*, June, 1953, contains the best discussion of this phase of the subject in the article "Do Silent Witnesses Defend Civil Liberties?" by Alan F. Westin. I commend it to Professor Einstein and his followers.

on the ground that such inquiries are themselves offenses against justice and freedom. He accepted the right to claim protection under the Fifth Amendment. He would, however, have the intellectual speak openly as a citizen in support of what he believes.

Dr. Einstein's motives in writing thus to a New York high-school teacher who had refused to answer questions regarding his communist affiliations were admirable. But the great scientist missed a basic fact and is ill-advised in his estimate of tactics. The basic fact is that the teacher was asked about his *act* of allegiance to the Communist Party, a conspiratorial organization, not about his personal opinions. I respectfully doubt whether the passionate anti-Nazi, the scientist most responsible for giving the world the atom bomb in the war against Hitler, would have given the same advice a few years ago to a teacher asked about his connection with a Nazi bund.

In any case his reasoning does not support his contention that individuals should constitute themselves final judges of what questions are proper in legislative inquiries and that by so doing they can commend freedom of belief and speech to their fellows. Would it not be far more effective for the individual to protest the inquiry, but then, by answering questions, assert his willingness to justify his beliefs on important matters in the court of public opinion?

Educational authorities in some states are compelled by law to discharge teachers in schools or colleges under public control who refuse to answer questions concerning their connection with communism. At Harvard University, which is not under similar compulsion of law, the Corporation severely rebuked, but did not discharge, three teachers who refused to testify before investigating committees and claimed protection under the Fifth Amendment. The *Christian Science Monitor* in an authoritative article on "The Campus and the Congressman," June 1, 1953, thus described the Harvard position: "Harvard considers present membership in the Communist Party almost certain grounds for removal. But, satisfied that a man is no Communist, the Harvard policy is that 'no general rule will be applied to cases in which members of our teaching staff invoke the Fifth Amendment, but . . . each case will be decided on its merits after full and deliberate consideration of the facts and issues involved'."

I should support the position of the authorities of Harvard University concerning the best way to deal with this matter on the college campuses. It will be hard to apply on the public-school level. As has been pointed out in a previous chapter, the chief danger to democracy and the pursuit of truth by reason of communist interpenetration lies there rather than on the college level. That danger, and the related evils of McCarthyism, will be examined again in the discussion of local laws and community attitudes.

My third category of criticism of congressional inquiries is directed against the political grandstanding for personal fame of many of the committee chairmen. Dies, with the aid of his ex-communist (or devout fellow-trav-

eler) research man J. B. Matthews, whose public morals
were not improved when he renounced communism, compiled the widely circulated Appendix 9 to his Committee
report without specific appropriations for it from his Committee or specific authorization for it. It is now almost un-
available to the public, but it bobs up in all sorts of places
when it can be used to discredit one of the 25,000 names
allegedly listed in it. It is charged that Matthews on quit-
ting his office as chief investigator took with him a great
many copies for his own use and that Martin Dies did the
same.

In the current investigations, Velde has been criticized
by some of his colleagues in the House for talking too much
about what his Committee would do. McCarthy has exercised himself, not always successfully, to browbeat certain
witnesses and to manipulate the occasional use of television
to his advantage. Television can be an invaluable servant
of the public, but manipulated in its use by chairmen who
choose what witnesses shall be heard and seen over it, and
on what subjects, in hearings not conducted under a proper
code, it can be an agency of serious persecution of the
individual.

In July, 1953, McCarthy brought upon himself well-
deserved rebuke from his own Committee when he decided
to employ the aforementioned J. B. Matthews, of Dies Committee fame, as a kind of director. The chairman acted on
his own authority. Immediately thereafter, an article by
Matthews appeared in the *American Mercury,* sounding a

frantic alarm over the extent of communist fellow-traveling and communist influence among the Protestant clergy. This brought dissatisfaction with McCarthy's tactics as chairman to a head. The Democratic members of his Committee resigned. They persisted in withdrawing even after Matthews resigned or declined his post. No other Democratic senators would serve, so that McCarthy's became strictly a Republican committee.

IX.

Loyalty and Security Tests

WHEN I BEGAN to draft this chapter at the end of May, 1953, our United States was allegedly the safer because: (1) Julius and Ethel Rosenberg awaited death as atom spies; (2) Mrs. Mildred McAfee Horton, former commander of the WAVES, former president of Wellesley, active in the National Council of Churches, one of the ablest women in America, had not been cleared in time by the State Department to accept an important appointment for which the President had designated her; (3) Stuart Morris, a distinguished and uncompromising British pacifist, had been denied admission to the country at Ellis Island, although he had been cleared for admission by our consular authorities in England: his visa was merely a ticket of admission to our concentration camp on the island;

(4) Walter Bergman, high in the educational system of Detroit, a visiting lecturer in Denmark, a lifelong socialist and no communist, had his passport summarily lifted in Denmark, on the ground that somebody or other had once said he was a communist.*

Thus did our omniscient bureaucracy guard and protect the brave and the free in the land of the pioneers, of Jefferson, Lincoln, and the Bill of Rights.

Strictly speaking, the Rosenberg case does not belong in this book on civil liberty. On its agonizingly tortuous course through our courts, fair-minded and honorable judges found no adequate reason to reject the jury's verdict finding the Rosenbergs guilty of active participation in an atom spy ring. At all stages the right of the Rosenbergs to appeal and of their sympathizers to protest was protected. The final justice of these courts' decisions was somewhat clouded by the belief of three judges of the standing of Justices Douglas, Black, and Frankfurter that there was some doubt concerning which law the Rosenbergs were convicted under.† It was, I thought, a pity, in terms of public policy, that the Supreme Court did not grant a full and open hearing on the merits of the case as well as which law

---

* Mr. Bergman's passport at long—and expensive—last was unconditionally restored in October, 1953.

† The question of the applicability of the law to the Rosenbergs, which won a stay from Justice Douglas, was raised by a radical and erratic lawyer from California named Irwin Edelman, who had recently been expelled from the Los Angeles Committee to Secure Justice for the Rosenbergs, nominally a nonpartisan committee but really, as Edelman's expulsion for differing from some communist comrades conclusively showed, subservient to the party.

was applicable to it. But the case for the innocence of the
Rosenbergs was exceedingly weak; it was never established
as was the innocence of Sacco and Vanzetti. What I, like
thousands of others, urged on President Truman and later,
through Attorney General Brownell, on President Eisenhower, was a commutation of sentence. I believed the
Rosenbergs guilty. But although their abhorrent conspiracy
continued years after World War II, the overt acts of which
the Rosenbergs were found guilty were committed to aid
an ally during the war; no other atom spy was dealt with
so severely; public opinion, cleverly exploited by communists, here and abroad, was shocked by the severity of the
sentence—a reaction heightened emotionally by the fact
that it was imposed on the mother of two young children.
President Eisenhower's refusal to commute the sentence
gave the communists the martyrs they wanted. My own
experience in working with communists and others, in the
thirties, in the defense of Athos Terzani, a victim of Art
Smith's Khaki Shirts, who tried to frame him for murder,
taught me that communists prefer unjust convictions or
convictions which can be exploited rather than acquittals
at the hands of "capitalist" courts. I reminded Attorney
General Brownell of the Terzani case and its aftermath.

Now the communists need never fear that the Rosenbergs will talk; they have the given fact of a sentence of
terrible severity, a fact which they will continue to em-
broider with falsehoods, including charges of anti-Semitism
in our courts. They will continue to use the case to divert

attention from their own unnumbered abominations committed in the name of law in Russia, China, and the satellite countries. Judge Kaufman and President Eisenhower were guilty of the popular error of confusing severity of vengeance with justice, in this case at the expense of the national interest. As matters turned out, even the safeguards of the right of repeated appeal, a feature in American criminal procedure without parallel elsewhere, served only to prolong the agony and give the communists a chance to do their propaganda job.

The cases of Mrs. Horton, Stuart Morris, and Walter Bergman, which illustrate the government's concern over the character of those who seek to enter, or to leave, or to serve our country, are of a different order. Better judgment has already partially repaired the damage done by overzealous officials. None other than Undersecretary of State Walter Bedell Smith, in a curious sort of way, apologized to Mrs. Horton. Through a letter to Senator Jackson, of Washington, he made the humiliating confession that his department, under its new regime of Republican big-business efficiency, was so bound up in its own red tape that it couldn't act in time to clear Mrs. Horton for the conference to which the President had wished to send her. There were plenty of cynics who thought that fear of McCarthy and the presence of Scott McLeod, guardian of official purity in the Department itself, were at least equally powerful explanations of the insult to a distinguished American.

Mr. Stuart Morris, after a brief stay in Ellis Island, was admitted for a sixty-day visit and speaking tour, by the action of the Appeals Board with the concurrence of the Attorney General. The Board's decision was prompt and admirable in its reasoning. Perhaps it will serve to prevent a repetition of Mr. Morris' experience.

The English visitor fared better than the American traveler. It was fifty days after Walter Bergman's passport had been taken from him in Copenhagen before he received the formal, official statement of the charges against him. The only one that was serious (unless we are to believe that no one should travel who doesn't agree with Senator McCarthy or Scott McLeod), was the allegation that Mr. Bergman in 1943 had belonged to the Communist Party. The source of the allegation was not given, and Mr. Bergman in Copenhagen was confronted with no witness. Those of us who know the man and his record believed the charge to be completely false. His passport was ultimately restored but with restrictions limiting its validity to specific nations. He returned home and was still fighting for complete clearance as this chapter was finished. This expensive and humiliating experience for the victim does the United States nothing but harm among our friends in Scandinavian countries, in which Walter Bergman was becoming well known and respected. Mr. Bergman's experience is typical of the difficulties of those suddenly confronted with charges of disloyalty by witnesses whose very names are unknown to the accused.

Mrs. Horton's case turned the spotlight on the Eisenhower administration's loyalty and security policy in respect to personnel. All nominees for office and all civil service employees must be name-checked, and a great many must be screened. This is a continuation, with some changes, of policy initiated by President Truman. Security procedures are authorized under Public Law 733, giving the employees some protection but granting great discretionary power on procedure to the President.

One would like to dismiss this subject by saying that any sort of security screening is unnecessary. Unfortunately, that can't be done in view of the record of communist interpenetration in the government. In addition to the better-known cases already mentioned, the record shows that communists in the post office at one time stole considerable mail passing between Leon Trotsky, then in Mexico, and his followers in the United States. During our honeymoon with the communists they gained important posts in the Office of Strategic Services (OSS), special guardian of our country.

The questions that arise are these: Who should be screened—every officeholder, or only candidates for sensitive positions in which disloyalty or plain untrustworthiness can do special harm? What are sensitive positions? How should they be determined? What rights should be given employees or candidates for employment?

There is no easy answer to these questions. As the story of Trotsky's experience with the mail suggests, the definition of sensitive positions is extraordinarily difficult. A government chauffeur may overhear very confidential conversations between men whom he is driving. Obviously some positions in private employment on special government contracts, in communications, or in shipping, can be more sensitive than most government jobs.

The problem certainly cannot be solved by screening everyone. The burden of work for anything like a proper screening would be intolerable. There are thousands of jobs where the opportunity for successful espionage or sabotage is so inconsiderable, compared with the risk involved, as to make the jobs immune to danger of communist or fascist conspiracy whatever the political opinions of their holders. The Eisenhower administration has recognized this fact by requiring only a routine name check for a great many positions. Full-scale screening will be required only for sensitive positions, a class into which all positions in the State Department have been placed. In other departments also, departmental security officers have power to designate positions as sensitive. Moreover, except where there may be hearings on actual charges, these officers have practically unrestricted power to determine who will fill sensitive posts below the high political policy-making level. It is reported that many security officers, desiring to play it safe and avoid controversy, overclassify sensitive positions and then inform the incumbents that they must resign, face charges, or be transferred to non-sensitive positions, often at a loss of civil service standing and pay. Add to this the fact that wholesale discharges under the economy program are in process, and you have a picture of a situation in which civil service morale is badly undermined.

Scott McLeod, security officer in the State Department, is on record as determined to use all his influence and power to put and keep socialists out of his department, at least in positions affecting policy—this although he does not challenge their loyalty. Harold Stassen's record of dismissals from his Department of Foreign Operations strongly suggests a like purpose. He and Mr. McLeod both seem to regard active New Dealers as equivalent to socialists and to believe that almost any position under their control is in some sense policy-making. Actions such as these of McLeod and Stassen mark the end of civil service independent of party politics.

Under the Eisenhower rules the loyalty and security programs are formally combined. This theoretically, and one hopes in practice, means (1) that more and more of the decisions made by security officers will be determined by actual security needs and will not involve assessments of motives to the degree required by the loyalty decisions; and (2) that dismissal will carry less danger of punishment by imputation of disloyalty than formerly existed. It is unfortunately probable that the disloyalty angle of this sort of inquiry is so impressed on the public mind that most people will be suspicious of every discharged civil servant.

All this makes vital to a sound civil service and decent

regard for individual right several changes, among which a fairer, more objective classification of sensitive positions is perhaps most important. One suggestion has been made which I should endorse. It is that a panel of experts be set up under the Civil Service Commission to which departments should be required to submit their recommendations for classifying positions as sensitive. The decision of this body should be binding and should be a matter of public record.

Further protection should also be given to individuals against whom formal charges may be filed. Before President Truman introduced his loyalty procedures, I had urged that the whole question of loyalty and procedures to deal with disloyalty be examined by a committee of distinguished citizens. The President preferred to set up immediately a cumbersome screening process, which did, however, provide more opportunity for appeals than the Eisenhower program has allowed.

In Mr. Truman's administration very few employees were discharged for disloyalty, and I doubt if any of them were improperly discharged. But many civil servants were compelled to undergo protracted and very expensive hearings. So clumsy were procedures that men cleared in their respective departments had to undergo the same experience all over again in transfer to other jobs. There were cases in which an employee would be cleared only to have fresh charges brought against him by nameless individuals, perhaps personal enemies, who were never identified to him. One man whom I had known at a certain period of his life and to whom I had given an affidavit had to undergo this process of proving his loyalty three times. At the end he was cleared, but the proceedings dragged out over a number of years and cost, he told me, some $20,000, his own and his wife's life savings. I have heard of cases in which there was suspicion that the renewed charges were made, under the cloak of secrecy which protects informers, by communists (not known as such) against ex-communists who had renounced the Party. It would appeal to communists thus to manipulate the government to punish their enemies.

The government holds that it must protect sources of information and therefore cannot let the accused confront certain accusers. I reluctantly grant a certain weight to the argument. All the more need, then, to give the accused every possible right to confront his accusers and all other possible protections. Some further suggestions for such protection are these:

1. Hearing boards should not be designated from within government departments by department heads. They should be appointed by federal courts from distinguished members of the bar or others with special qualifications who are not themselves dependent upon the favor of department heads for their jobs or promotions.

2. Such boards should be allowed greater latitude than now exists to examine allegedly "confidential" informants on whose testimony charges are sometimes based.

3. When loyalty is not directly involved but only the competence or trustworthiness of a particular individual for a particular job, hearing boards should be allowed to recommend transfer to less sensitive jobs.

4. The employee should not be suspended, as now, as soon as formal charges are brought against him. He should be continued at his work for a reasonable time in which to prepare his defense, but denied access to classified material. Time limits should be imposed within which the accusers must present their case and the defendant be prepared to meet it.

Somewhat analogous procedures should be established for screening employees of private corporations occupying real or allegedly sensitive positions. I shall comment briefly in a later chapter on some aspects of screening for private employment which have come to my attention. In general, complaints on this score have been very few in these times of relatively full employment.

One cannot discuss loyalty or security procedures in public or private employment without giving attention to the Attorney General's list of subversive organizations. The principle of no listing without a hearing or opportunity for a hearing was not fairly applied, but the Attorney General's list as it now stands is composed mostly, though not entirely, of organizations which at one time or other were communist or fascist fronts. However, on its face, the list sheds no light on such problems as these: How important was the organization listed? Is it still in existence? What innocent or praiseworthy end did it profess to serve? Was it started by communists or captured by them? If originally noncommunist, at what point in time did it become communist-dominated?

If the list were properly classified under headings answering these questions it would be easier for security screeners to weigh the importance of a man's connection with the organization. Did he ever really join it? Did he attend its meetings or sign its petitions? Or did he merely attend some meeting it promoted or sign some letter it circulated because he was in sympathy with the avowed purpose of the meeting, letter, or petition? If he was an active member, at what stage of its history? Did he, perhaps, like many good men, stay for a time in a useful organization to try to prevent its going over to the communists?

I know at least two good men, leading anticommunists who were barred from government posts because of membership in organizations which were finally taken over by the communists, a fate against which they had fought in order to save a valuable organization, like the antifascist North American Committee to Aid Spanish Democracy, for service to its avowed purpose—which was not the advancement of communism.

The Attorney General's list, which lends itself to such easy abuse in government service, also has been employed effectively to injure men's reputations and to hurt them in private employment (for instance in motion pictures, radio,

television) and in the public schools. No attorney general
has exerted himself to prevent this misuse of the list. Its
existence and its abuse explain the extraordinary reluctance
that honest but timid folk—students, teachers, plain citizens—feel nowadays about signing anything or joining anything to the left of the American Medical Association, the
National Association of Manufacturers, or the Daughters
of the American Revolution. Why take a chance? If you do
nothing, there will be nothing on your record to hold
against you.

For this noxious growth of fear, liberals themselves
are partially to blame. They didn't get together intelli-
gently to fight, first communism, and then McCarthyism,
in or out of Congress. Not in time.

I hold liberal lawyers directly responsible for a share
of the difficulties besetting civil service employees tested
for security. They seem rather generally to have advised
their clients to play down any sentiments or actions in the
radical thirties which could be interpreted in the Mc-
Carthyist fifties as establishing some connection with communism. I myself gave evidence for two persons whose
lawyers went so far in playing down their sympathies in
the thirties as to promote reasonable suspicion that they—
who were never communists—were covering up something.
If at the beginning of security inquiries, honest men and
women had adopted generally the old-fashioned maxim,
Tell the truth and shame the devil, they would have cleared
the air and shortened their sufferings. Their answer should

have been not the weasel words suggested by their lawyers, but a frank statement: "Yes, in 1933 or thereabouts, I hoped much of the Russian Revolution, did not join the Communist Party but did not curse it, and sometimes worked with communists for a cause in which I believed. Later I learned the truth." They might have added: "Anyway, I never praised Stalin so indiscriminately as Wendell Willkie praised him on his return from discovering one world." They would have won more rapid understanding of the situation which was fairly general in the thirties.

My sympathies are less with some of the more prominent slaves to a fear they might have helped to fight by candor and courage than with less prominent people whose exaggerated terror, unsupported, I grant, by the facts, is nevertheless one of the saddest and most ruinous products of the psychological identification of McCarthyism with Americanism.

Let me illustrate. The Workers Defense League, *not* an organization on the Attorney General's list, has been giving legal aid to aliens threatened with deportation under the McCarran Act. It sent out an appeal letter which I signed. The response was generous, but it gave the most poignant evidence of popular fear that I had seen. One contribution was received from a person who signed himself "A Coward," with no other name. Fifteen other contributions were sent in in cash with no identifying names. One note, enclosing five dollars, read as follows: "It is surely the most pertinent comment on our growing communism—

that is, authoritarianism—that my husband and I are afraid to sign our names to this. But here are five of our carpenter dollars and if our despair gets much worse will send you our total savings of $1,677."

The deportation cases for which I was appealing and which evoked such disquieting replies tend to illustrate the tendency to protect Americans by making ours a quasi-hermit nation in respect to personal contact with foreigners whose views may displease Senators McCarthy and Mc-Carran.

The State Department has used its authority under law to deny or lift a considerable number of passports, and to delay intolerably the granting of others. The theory is, of course, that this denial is in the interest of our national security—the same theory which, expressed in the McCar-ran-Walter Act, gives consular officials abroad, and immigration authorities at home, such broad powers to screen immigrants and alien visitors. It is a ridiculous and humiliating performance illustrative of a lack of internal confidence in our own democracy, a lack which is increased by the inevitable tendency of bureaucrats to expand their powers.

For instance, a passport was denied to Corliss Lamont. Although I strongly criticize his defense of communism, it seems patent to me that unless the State Department has reason that it has never revealed to believe him a communist courier—an absurd assumption—the denial of his passport can be far more harmful to our reputation abroad than can any speeches he might make. Denied a citizen's privilege, he can also commend himself and his ideas the better here at home to the discontented. Not even Senator McCarthy has suggested a concentration camp for Mr. Lamont. If he can travel at home, why not abroad? Denying him a passport does not bottle up his opinions or news of them.

As for alien visitors and immigrants, the McCarran-Walter Act, which codified our scattered laws governing immigration and naturalization, is, despite some improvements over laws it superseded, as a whole a living monument to the defeat of American liberalism in spirit and in tactics. It could not have been passed over President Truman's veto except for accident and the gross miscalculation of its liberal opponents, who supposedly had enough votes to sustain the veto.

The Act has been denounced repeatedly and ably for its rigid quotas based on calculations of race and national origin which cannot be justified by principles of science or religion. Of special concern in the discussion of civil liberty is the evidence the McCarran-Walter Act gives of a fearful spirit in America which is in complete reversal of the spirit by which our fathers built the nation. We fear contamination not only by prospective immigrants but even by alien visitors, and to protect ourselves we give to a governmental bureaucracy powers unknown to nations which don't boast as much as we of individual freedom.

Section 212 (27) of the Act sums up these powers in

listing among the nonadmissible: "Aliens who the consular officer or Attorney General knows or has reason to believe seek to enter the United States solely, principally or incidentally, to engage in activities which could be prejudicial to the public interest or endanger the welfare, safety, or security of the United States." Under this and similar provisions excluding anarchists, communists, and other subversives, visitors and prospective immigrants have to be cleared by both the consular authority abroad (a State Department official) and the immigration authorities (under the Department of Justice) here in America. And as Stuart Morris discovered, it isn't enough to win approval by one authority. It is fortunate that the reviewing authority under Mr. Brownell made a good ruling in the Morris case.

To give the law its due, some provisions are better than parts of the older laws which it replaced. For instance, the earlier McCarran Act gave no room for repentance to any former totalitarian. The present law will admit repentant totalitarians five years after their change of heart if they have "actively opposed" the doctrine they once accepted. Says the ACLU:

> This section should be broadened to permit the entry of former totalitarians, who repudiate the ideology under oath. The bill is restrictive, too, in requiring the deportation of any alien who, at any time after admission, had been active in Communist or totalitarian political causes. This is regardless of whether such a mistake was acknowledged and the association terminated. The same criticism should be leveled at the section which

renders deportable any alien who once was associated with activities "prejudicial to the public interest," even if such actions had long since ceased and frequently even if such associations were innocently made. Fear and lack of understanding of the principle of change, both in history and human life, is characterized by the section disqualifying from citizenship any person who was once affiliated with the "direct predecessor" of a Communist or totalitarian organization, despite the fact that the original groups may have been democratic in nature and the individual had resigned in protest when it was captured by Communist forces.

The law in other sections gives the attorney general undue discretionary powers of deportation for all sorts of reasons. Both President Eisenhower and Adlai Stevenson criticized the law during the campaign of 1952; a great many social agencies have denounced various of its important features. The screening of sailors under the law has irritated our friends, Norwegian, British, and French. That particular evil has been minimized by sensible procedural administration. But no steps have been taken in Congress for drastic amendment of the law itself, which is a betrayal of the great American tradition.

Not only are aliens and American government employees involved in American loyalty procedures, but the United Nations itself. That organization employs many Americans in its work, which supposedly is above nationalism. Belatedly our government is applying screening processes to American applicants for, or holders of, UN civil service positions. It is true that the UN's civil service should be kept outside national politics. But that principle does not conflict logically with the right of the American government—or any other—to try to prevent the employment of members or adherents of a conspiratorial policy opposed to it in positions where unquestionably they can hurt its interests, if not endanger its security. *That is, if it is adherence to a conspiratorial movement and not political dissent which is involved.* The UN is not a government resting upon universal citizenship, but a glorified alliance of nations. At first, our government took too little interest in the true allegiance of Americans who sought UN posts. Then came grandstand investigation and a very awkwardly handled exchange over the issue with the UN. Now the President has decreed screenings of American applicants under a special review board, with recognition that the ultimate decision is with the UN. If Senator McCarran has his way, an American applicant who does not accept this American screening and takes employment under the UN will be subject to fine and imprisonment. This law would so outrage sentiment in the UN, which must act as master in its own house, that even the State Department, with all its fear of McCarthy and McCarran, opposes its passage. The issue has been made more acute by the ruling of a UN board that certain employees were improperly discharged by former Secretary Lie for refusing to answer questions put them by a congressional committee concerning their communist connections. Good sense all around should avoid a conflict hurtful alike to the US and the UN.

X.

McCarthyism at State and Local Levels

ON THE MORNING of May 12, 1953, I, along with thousands of residents of Baltimore and other visitors to the city, opened the newspaper to discover that police checkers from the office of the attorney general had scrutinized all who attended a meeting at the Lyric Theatre the night before under the auspices of the World Federalists, an organization apparently suspect to ardent McCarthyites. Governor McKeldin of Maryland rebuked the attorney general's office and apologized for the state. That's the good side of the story. But the names apparently were filed. If not these names, then others similarly gathered have apparently been filed, so that the state may be better able to carry out its antisubversive law, the Ober Act.

Neither on my brief visit in Maryland nor since have

I discerned any burning popular indignation to match the Governor's at this sort of police state activity. Perhaps one reason is that although Maryland is one of the great majority of American states having some sort of law or laws dealing with subversive movements and parties (mostly aimed at communists), the ACLU in its report covering the situation through 1952 could cite no single prosecution of an individual under these laws, except in Pennsylvania, where a communist leader, Steve Nelson, was convicted under a sedition statute. (He has since been convicted under the Smith Act.) Later Professor Dirk Struit was indicted under a Massachusetts statute. Prosecutions were pending in Louisiana and California under laws requiring public registration of subversive organizations and their members. In 1953 the Trucks registry law in Michigan was attacked in the courts.

Michigan in 1950 went to the shocking length of imposing life imprisonment as a penalty for writing or speaking subversive words, and the ACLU reports that Tennessee in 1951 "adopted a law calling for the death penalty in cases of unlawful advocacy." It is indeed fortunate that there have been no prosecutions under such laws.

While the states have generally left actual prosecution of allegedly seditious individuals to the federal government, they have more or less effectively enforced penalties against "subversive" organizations. According to the ACLU report, the record shows:

Twenty-six states with laws barring from the ballot any subversive political organization, defined to reach Communists; some make such organizations criminal; effectiveness of the laws in practice varies.

Eleven states with laws denying use of schools as meeting places to subversive organizations; enforcement is effective.

Five states with laws requiring subversive organizations and their members to register . . . no one has registered.

Two states, Pennsylvania and Massachusetts, in 1952 adopted laws making membership in an organization advocating overthrow of the government a crime, thus, in effect, outlawing the Communist Party; not yet enforced! . . .

The few test cases taken into the courts have on the whole sustained the state anti-subversive laws in principle.

The ACLU report verifies what is probably the general impression, namely, that the chief activity of states with reference to individuals has been in the enactment and enforcement of special loyalty oaths. All but six states require special oaths for teachers, or for all public employees, or for civil-defense workers. Eight states, including New York, California, Ohio, and Indiana, have "all three kinds of laws." In California a special oath for teachers imposed by the Regents was declared unconstitutional. The Supreme Court of the United States found a particular oath exacted of Oklahoma employees unconstitutional because retroactive.

California, Washington, Illinois, Ohio, Massachusetts, New Hampshire, and New Jersey have had "un-American" activities committees. Arizona and Florida appointed committees which did not function. The New Jersey committee has functioned only in closed meetings. Governor Adlai Stevenson vetoed laws passed by the legislature on recommendation of the Illinois committee although its own report, after investigation aimed in effect at the University of Chicago and Roosevelt College, showed that it found no seditious activities. In 1953 the Republican governor, Stratton, vetoed a silly and vicious bill which had passed the legislature.

The worst of these committees was California's, presided over from 1941 to 1949 by Jack Tenney. "So outlandish," says the ACLU, "were his activities that he was removed from his Committee and his bills killed. But his extensive listings generally have been taken over by the House un-American Activities Committee and are used both by public officials and private veteran and patriotic agencies to name people 'found to be communists or sympathizers by official government agencies'."

As for the special loyalty oaths, they have merely troubled and offended Quakers and others with tender consciences, disgusted scientists and others with special qualifications, and turned them from public employment. They have caught no secret communists. No well-trained communist would hesitate to take a loyalty oath to gain or hold a post his Party wanted him to hold. The fact that a teacher or other employee has taken some special oath may possibly make him more easily liable to prosecution for perjury —there has been none such in the educational field. Obviously loyalty oaths deter the timid liberal rather than the dangerous subversive. It is insulting to decent Americans to be singled out for special loyalty oaths beyond the well-accepted general oaths properly taken by all public officials. The popularity of these special oaths with legislators (and presumably their constituents) attests an attitude of irrational suspicion, soothed by verbal incantations.

Loyalty oaths are part of the story of the effort to prevent subversive activities in our schools, which fall far more directly under state than federal control. I have argued in earlier chapters that I do not believe that communists, or other totalitarians, should teach in our public schools—at least not until future changes in communist policy result in a definite change of its purpose and method of achieving universal power, or offer proof of American communist independence of the Kremlin and abandonment of conspiratorial tactics.

The university situation is of itself much more easily manageable on rational lines than the situation in areas (not too numerous) where communists have interpenetrated the grade schools. There is little evidence to warrant alarm over communism in the university world. Educators differ somewhat in their announced opinions on whether adherence to the communist line should in itself debar a professor from a college or university post. They would in overwhelming majority agree with Sidney Hook that faculties are the best judges of the loyalty of their fellow teachers.

The situation is far more complex in the few cities like New York where unquestionably there was and probably still is considerable communist interpenetration in the public schools. State legislation in New York forbids the employment of communists as teachers. But the law in question (the Devaney Law) defined no standards. It was later supplemented by the Feinberg Law, authorizing the Regents to set up a list of subversive organizations for the guidance of local authorities. The process was attended with many safeguards and, as this was written, still was incomplete. New York City, under a local law affecting city employees, makes discharge mandatory for teachers who will not answer questions on their totalitarian connections. Therefore teachers are slowly being discharged under the law, which for various reasons is now challenged in the courts. Most states trust loyalty oaths to protect them from communist teachers.

It would, I think, be enough to empower and instruct local boards to discharge, or to refuse to hire, communists, defined as adherents of a conspiratorial movement, *not as holders of unorthodox opinions.* From a local decision, a teacher under sentence of dismissal should be permitted to appeal, under specified conditions, to the highest educational authority in the state.

Few, if any, teachers will acknowledge adherence to communism. (Those who would are obviously the least dangerous.) Hence the question of proof becomes all-important. And very bothersome, the more so because of the organized effort to label any expression of opinion to the left, let us say, of Governor Thomas E. Dewey, as evidence of communism.

Some advocates of the theory that a teacher should be discharged only on proof of attempted communist indoctrination in the classroom assign the difficulty of proving adherence to the Communist Party as a reason for their position. Sidney Hook points out corresponding and possibly greater difficulties in gathering proof of actual or attempted indoctrination in the classroom. Persons, justly or unjustly suspicious of the teacher, confined to "getting something on him" in the classroom, might set up veritable amateur detective rings in the schoolroom, enlisting the children and completely disrupting the school's morale. Is it not probable (1) that legal acknowledgment of the principle that members of a totalitarian conspiracy are disqualified from teaching in our schools may quiet some fearful souls now made apprehensive by the liberals' defense of the right of such persons to teach, and (2) that evidence concerning communist adherence may be obtained by considering the general range of a teacher's activities with more total fairness to the accused and less disruption in the school than by intense concentration on the classroom?

(I have previously argued that an able communist teacher or a Ku Kluxer can do a lot of harm without easily being caught in specific indoctrination in the classroom.)

As I write there is no evidence warranting a general anticommunist crusade in our public schools and little evidence of attempts to discharge teachers as communists. Discharges of teachers, as recorded in Chapter VIII, have usually been for their refusal to answer questions put to them by a local or congressional investigating committee and their claim of protection under the Fifth Amendment. Not the number of discharges, but the atmosphere of suspicion and timidity that has been created has injured our school system.

The case histories of troubles in our schools usually involve directly local rather than state-wide attacks on the way they are conducted, the textbooks they use, and the chief administrators whom the school boards employ. Charges of communism, socialism, or internationalism—all virtually synonymous to the complainants—have been indiscriminately thrown in. Unofficial prejudice, stupidity, and self-interest, even more than federal or state action against communism, is responsible for the alarming furor stirred up concerning school and library systems, textbooks and books on library shelves in towns and cities as widely separated as Los Angeles and Pasadena, California, Englewood, New Jersey, Scarsdale and Port Washington, New York, Houston and San Antonio, Texas, Sapulpa, Oklahoma, Indianapolis, Indiana, and New Haven, Connecticut—to name the better-known cases. Yet this furor ties in with the complex we call McCarthyism. It is encouraged by what is said and done in Washington. Sooner or later, the cry of communism has been raised to damn not only democratic socialism and the welfare state but all sorts of things from progressive education and UNESCO to Professor Einstein's theory of relativity.

The disgraceful stories of what happened in Pasadena to Superintendent Willard E. Goslin, or of the campaign in Los Angeles which led the Board of Education to ban the pamphlet *The E in UNESCO*, prepared by the school administrators to explain UNESCO to the teachers, do not belong in detail to this book because they involved other factors besides anticommunist hysteria.

In many cities there is legitimate concern about the kind and quality of public-school education. Honest and public-spirited citizens have a right to question whether under progressive education sufficient attention is paid to content—spelling, arithmetic, American history, for instance. They have a right to a concern over the way textbooks present facts and opinions to the pupils. The trouble has been that too often this concern has been exploited by superheated patriots who attribute statements they do not like—or understand—to socialism and communism.

They attack the administration in schools as red or pink. They demand the exclusion of certain textbooks from the curriculum, and they constitute themselves censors over the books in public and school libraries. While the activi-

ties are usually carried on locally under the leadership of
some more or less prominent citizen or group of citizens, a
number of national organizations excite and exploit these
local fears and prejudices. One of the worst is the National
Council for American Education, organized and headed
by Allen A. Zoll. I quote from an admirable article in *Commentary* (February, 1952) by Edward N. Saveth, entitled
"What to Do about 'Dangerous' Textbooks?" He writes:

> Allen A. Zoll . . . has come up from the ranks of the
> chauvinist, isolationist, and anti-Semitic agitators of the
> 1930's and 1940's to emerge as a full-fledged authority
> on education in 1952. Zoll's old organization, American
> Patriots, Inc., was included in the December 1947 At-
> torney General's list of "totalitarian, fascist, Communist,
> or subversive" organizations. His new outfit, organized
> to exploit whatever pickings the educational field has to
> offer, nearly died aborning when Frederick Woltman's
> article, "Zoll, Hatemonger, Promotes New Racket," ap-
> peared in the New York *World-Telegram* on August 25,
> 1948; the article led to the resignation of General Jona-
> than Wainwright and Gene Tunney from the organiza-
> tion's governing board. Yet, despite the exposé of Zoll's
> activities, his organization was still effective enough to
> contribute substantially to the ouster of the progressive
> educator Dr. Willard E. Goslin from his post as superin-
> tendent of Pasadena's schools. His denunciatory reviews
> of textbooks which do not conform to his own perverted
> standards of Americanism have been used in attacks
> upon specific titles in Englewood, New Jersey, and else-
> where.

Another active organization in the same field is the
Conference of American Small Business Organizations,

which somehow or other would connect the success of small business with inculcation of small ideas of patriotism and with distortion of fact.

This organization has a committee on education which publishes the *Educational Reviewer*, devoted almost entirely to reviews of textbooks and teaching material, all in the interest of "the American system." The editor, a woman of some ability named Lucille Cardin Crain, proved her effectiveness by her attack on Frank A. Magruder's *American Government*, the most widely used textbook in its field. Her magazine's biased, inaccurate, and distorted review of the book was picked up by radio commentator Fulton Lewis, Jr., after which the book was banned throughout Georgia and in cities in various parts of the country.

Liberals are justly outraged by this sort of banning of textbooks, yet it must be said that not all liberals come to the court of public opinion with clean hands. The Teachers Union in New York, which poses as the champion of liberalism—outside the iron curtain—demanded that some twenty-odd books whose attitudes towards immigrant and minority groups it professed to find objectionable should be "scrapped or corrected" by the New York Board of Education. The NAACP protested the use of the college textbook *The Growth of the American Republic* by Samuel Eliot Morison of Harvard and Henry Steele Commager of Columbia, usually considered liberal and well-informed historians, because this generally admirable organization

thought the book offered a biased treatment of the Negro
as slave and freed man.

Obviously, the question of what textbooks to use in our
schools cannot be decided offhand, especially since there
are so many controversial points of view concerning history
and economics. By and large, however, the process of selecting textbooks is so carefully handled that objection to
particular books, as communist on the one hand, and as
reactionary on the other, must be well established by fact.
Such factual proof is rarely offered by the critics. Publishers
are usually more anxious to sell new books than to defend
textbooks under attack. Teachers have shown a little more
courage. By and large it is the teaching profession which
should judge the books used as texts in the school, and the
community should support them except in cases where
fair and decisive proof of bias or prejudice can be submitted
in orderly fashion to the educational authorities.

While justification can be pleaded for public concern
over the textbooks used in schools, there is no justification
at all for the book burning, quite in the Hitlerian spirit,
which has begun to disgrace America. President Eisenhower himself at the Dartmouth commencement denounced book burning in the true Jeffersonian spirit. It
was immensely regrettable that a few days later he weakened the force of his remarks by justifying or partially justifying the book-burning show put on by his own State Department in American information centers abroad. The
history of this humiliating scandal is briefly this:

Joe McCarthy, who from afar had learned of heresy in our information centers abroad, finally sent two of his brash young men, Messrs. Cohn and Schine, to Europe, where to the irritated amusement of literate Europeans, they put on a show of smelling out bad books on the shelves of our information centers. The boys came home and told McCarthy their horrid findings. McCarthy, Grand Inquisitor and Thought Controller by grace of the Republican Party, shook a monitory finger (or club) in the direction of the State Department, which in a dither of anticipatory fright had already begun to send out a series of confused directives to purge our libraries of controversial books by controversial authors. One directive was said to be responsible for removing three hundred titles by eighteen authors, sixteen of whom had refused to testify. Local authorities, no heroes, confused by the State Department's confusion and wanting to be on the safe side, threw out no one knows how many more. The score was in the hundreds of books, the works of at least forty authors, the majority of them American of loyalty and distinction. For a time it looked as if the FBI would have to conduct a full-scale loyalty inquiry into a man named Clemens, who used the alias Mark Twain. Actually thrown out from at least a few of our libraries were selected works of Thomas Paine, because they happened to be edited by Howard Fast, allegedly a communist; *As We See Russia*, by members of the Overseas Press Club, whose members aren't communists; a number of books by the Nobel Prize Winner Pearl Buck; the Lynds' classics, *Middletown* and *Middletown in Transition;* and *Rising Wind*, by Walter White, who is the very effective anticommunist president of the NAACP.

Meanwhile the President made his fine speech against book burning. McCarthy said, in effect: "Who, me? I burned no books. Ask Mr. Dulles." The President then said that he hadn't meant McCarthy. The rest of the explanation added to confusion.

In the end, after irreparable harm had been done to American reputation and a bad precedent set in Washington for local book burnings, a very sensible directive (disapproved of by McCarthy) was sent over from the State Department. It pointed out, correctly, that our foreign libraries should be selective, not all-inclusive, and it admitted the propriety of excluding, but not burning, certain types of communist books. But it laid down a wise and tolerant basis of inclusion of controversial books, including certain types of books by communist authors. I was led to understand, during my 1953 travels in Europe and North Africa, that most of the books banned in the first fright were being quietly restored to the shelves.

Here at home, the city fathers of San Antonio, Texas, like some other officious citizens in other towns, decided to save the Texans from dangerous books. (The state legislature had set them an example by passing a law banning books holding Texas up to ridicule.) Actual book burning was not attempted, but the mayor, named Jack White, was reported as saying that the city council might consider branding all communist-written volumes in the public library. Which might constitute the best sort of invitation to read them. It remained, however, for the local chapter of that amazing organization The Minutewomen, in San Antonio, to attack the problem of book censorship in vigorous fashion. Their organizer drew up a list of about six hundred titles, including, according to *The New York Times,* "Professor Einstein's 'Theory of Relativity,' Louis Untermeyer's 'Treasury of American and British Poetry,' Dorothy Canfield Fisher's 'Fables for Parents,' and Chaucer's 'Canterbury Tales'." The *Times* editorially commented that "Mr. Chaucer has either been cleared by the proper congressional committee or just has been overlooked." His books, it appears, weren't listed, as you might suspect, because Chaucer, Canterbury, and communism all begin with the same letter, but because they were illustrated by Rockwell Kent, an excellent artist and a suspected fellow traveler.

The *Times* reported that opposition to this foolishness was growing in San Antonio. The same good news comes from many American towns and cities. For example, the schools and the school library in Scarsdale, New York, which had been subject to a well-organized attack, were declared free of organized communist infiltration by the education and school-budget committee of the Scarsdale Town Club after a year's study, and so far this point of view has prevailed in the community. Nevertheless, as the committee says, the attack on the school "brought unfavorable attention to the community, caused unwarranted divisions within Scarsdale, and tended to arouse latent religious bigotry" (*New York Times,* April 24, 1953).

On the good side of the ledger should be mentioned the fact recorded by the Educational Research Service of the National Education Association that never before has education been treated so seriously and well or in so many articles as within recent months in lay magazines of wide circulation. Admirable articles have appeared, for instance, in *McCall's,* the *Saturday Review,* and *Commentary* on the particular matters discussed here. The battle for reason and fair play has by no means been lost in our communities. But it is far from won.

XI.

Unions, Radio-TV, and Communist Suspects

STUDY OF THE AMERICAN SCENE has tended to confirm my original suspicion that community pressures, fear about jobs, and fear of social disapproval, are doing more damage to the Jeffersonian ideal than the direct acts of the government. There is, of course, a continual interaction between public opinion and governmental action. Vocal opinion demands that the government "do something." The government does something, like the passage and enforcement of the Smith Act, and what it does increases rather than allays public suspicion of possible subversives in our midst. It is, to repeat, highly significant that Joseph McCarthy did not enter the Senate as a convinced and bigoted crusader against a communism he does not understand. He, a shrewd demagogue, partly by calculation, partly perhaps

by the development of a common emotion, made himself
the champion and spokesman of a public which finds it easier and more emotionally satisfying to hunt for individual
communist devils than to understand and counteract the
forces that make for communism.

These more or less general reflections are a preface
to comment on two sorts of action against communists, by
organizations and individuals outside government, which
have had a powerful effect upon the Communist Party, its
adherents, and persons suspected of fellow-traveling in its
fifth column. I refer to labor-union action against communism and communists, and to blacklisting by employers,
especially in the field of mass communication.

By and large, the union drive against communist interpenetration and communist control has been justified by
the facts, and with few exceptions, it has achieved satisfac-
tory results without denying the basic liberties of the
workers. Blacklists or something of the sort by employers
show far more evidences of the McCarthyist attitude and
spirit, and have definitely tended to encourage a conformist
type of culture, in which a vigorous democracy cannot
flourish.

As I have already said, the communist interpenetration in the unions was once very considerable. At the end
of World War II, communists had managed to dominate
many important unions or sections of unions, especially
in the CIO. In the latter organization, Lee Pressman, general counsel, an able lawyer and a communist who has

since recanted, had great influence upon Philip Murray, president of the CIO and of the Steelworkers. The latter was by no means a communist, but for a long time he turned a deaf ear to any reports of Lee Pressman's communist line.

The CIO was organized during the period of the united front against fascism, and communists co-operated in the organization of the CIO unions. John L. Lewis, the first president of the CIO, was also president of the United Mine Workers, which carried in its constitution a prohibition of membership to communists. Nevertheless, Lewis used them in organizing campaigns. It is said, on apparently good authority, that he answered a critic of this use of communists by the somewhat cryptic statement: "When a man goes hunting, who gets the game? The man or the dog?" Lewis was sure that he was the man in the CIO until that organization and its members completely ignored his advice to support Wendell Willkie in 1940.

During the war, the zeal of communists for Russian military success made their leaders in the labor unions ultra-patriotic in preventing strikes. Nevertheless, before, during, and immediately after World War II, there were occasions on which rather obviously communist leaders sacrificed the interests of the union to the interests of the Party, and the tactics by which the communist minority took and held power in certain unions aroused a steadily mounting opposition. The cleavage between the interests of American labor and the interests of the communists became very marked as the cold war went on.

Even before that, as far back as 1937, I recall an instructive experience of my own with Lee Pressman. It was during the bitterly contested Little Steel strike. I was in Massillon, Ohio, a day or two after police, some of them special officers, led by a chief who had not been properly sworn in, had run amok on a Sunday night. Without provocation, they had attacked strikers who with their families were coming away from a Sunday-night picnic at union headquarters. Later they went around breaking down doors in the lodging houses where many of the steelworkers lived and ransacking their rooms. I was shown the physical evidences of destruction, and after talking with some of the local leaders, I agreed to urge the union to bring legal proceedings against the town for damages. I went to Pittsburgh, headquarters of the union, and fortune favored me. A friend brought Pressman to a meeting I was holding before I had an opportunity to report at the union office. I seized the opportunity to tell him the story of Massillon. I noticed his indifference. When I had finished, he did not reply to me at all on the union story but began to berate me because some weeks before, on my return from Russia and Spain, I had written and spoken very critically of the communists. He ignored my report and offer of help for his union because I was anticommunist. It was this sort of thing, repeated through the years, that helped to give the communist show away.

In 1947 and 1948, strong leaders, like Mike Quill of the Transport Workers Union and Joe Curran of the National Maritime Union, broke openly and vigorously with their communist friends. Philip Murray forced Pressman's resignation in the spring of 1948 and began a well-planned campaign to win control of the unions by alerting the majority, which in too many cases had been indifferent to communist domination. The campaign was a success, with a few important exceptions. Labor pretty successfully cleaned its own house of communist control, in most cases without penalizing individual workers by loss of jobs.

In general, union practice has followed a pattern of which the ACLU itself approves or to which it does not object. Many unions by their constitution, by-laws, or custom with the force of law, bar communists from office. A few bar them from membership. Most unions do not, at least as long as the suspects do not employ the tactics which originally got Communists in trouble.

It must be admitted that this dual standard of membership for members and officers sounds illogical and unfair. Nevertheless, it approximates the equities of the situation. It is through officers that communists shaped and controlled policies in unions, with primary attention to the Party interest. Of necessity, the Party control over the rank-and-file members was far looser. A communist working in a textile mill or in a coal mine is in a very different position than is a teacher who is a communist. Unlike the teacher, he is not denying the principle which should guide his work.

The goal of the American labor union is to create a

situation in which every worker must participate in the union which bargains for him. There is no ideological basis of membership, except that a worker in an industry should be a citizen in its organized union much as he is a citizen of the country in which he lives. The right of a communist to be out of jail implies the right to work, and in many cases one must belong to the union in order to have the right to work. The system, then, which does not bar communists from unions, or treats resolutions on that subject as dead letters, is well justified. Only overt acts against the union's well-being can possibly justify such severe penalty as expulsion from the union or denial of the right to join the union. But so long as the conspiratorial Communist Party asserts primacy of control over its members, no independent labor union concerned for its interest and unwilling to be subject to any political party can afford to put communists in responsible offices.

It is cause for satisfaction that the unions accomplished so much in asserting their independence of the communist movement without submitting to dependence on the government. It is sometimes argued that the Taft-Hartley Act helped the situation by requiring the officers of unions to take a noncommunist oath before the union was eligible to represent the workers in collective bargaining. This I doubt. It is true that under pressure of the law, certain leaders with communist affiliations finally took the oath. But circumstances suggest that their resignation from the Communist Party, if it took place at all, was purely formal.

One official, Ben Gold of the Furriers Union, is now under indictment for perjury in this connection. All in all, the requirement produced great irritation in labor ranks, the more so because there was no equivalent requirement for employers. Even Senator Taft before his death decided that the oath no longer was necessary. Some of the politicians who do not want to drop the oath contemplate an equivalent requirement for employers.

As I write, the most obvious ill consequence of the oath is to be seen in connection with a bitter and violent struggle over the organization of the miners in the Bradley mines near Widen, West Virginia. The miners had an independent union; some of them wanted to bring the operator under United Mine Workers contract. They struck and were powerfully backed by John L. Lewis. Others stayed at work under the independent union. Mr. Lewis could not ask for intervention of the National Labor Relations Board under the law to hold an election because he had refused to take the required oath and hence was debarred from the normal procedure. The alternative has been violence, indirectly the result of a provision of a law to catch communists. Patently, John L. Lewis is no communist. Nominally, at least, communists are barred from his union.

In an earlier chapter, I have admitted that some positions in private employment are as sensitive to security requirements as any government posts. They present an opportunity for sabotage even in time of peace. Therefore, some sort of screening has been set up for certain jobs or types of jobs—for instance, after the outbreak of the Korean war, for sailors. In the National Maritime Union, communists both orthodox and heretical had once been numerous and active. The president of the NMU, Joe Curran, who had sometimes seemed to be a strong pro-communist, appears to have used his influence with shipping companies and the government to bar certain critics of his policies on the ground that they were communists. To the credit of the screening authorities—officers of the coast guard—they gave fair hearing to the accused men and cleared several. By no means always are government authorities the chief villains in our picture.

There was at least one case that came to my knowledge in which the Bell Aircraft Company seems to have acted to persuade government authorities to bar a man from a position in which security was important for no better reason than that he had been an active leader in a bitter strike. Here again, a government appeal board reversed the decision. It was a proper action, even if the active displeasure of so powerful a union as the UAW-CIO was probably a factor in bringing it about.

By and large there is no record of employers' exploiting the communist charge to hurt individual workers, except in the fields of radio, television, and the movies. It is widely believed that there is today in these agencies of mass communication of entertainment and information a blacklist, of which the principal victims are the writers, artists, and actors listed in the notorious book *Red Channels*. It is certain that there is a rather suffocating atmosphere of suspicion and timidity in these fields even in Hollywood, where communist sympathy was once a popular fad.

In none of the other areas discussed in this book is it so difficult to be sure of one's facts. As Louis Berg says, and documents, in his able article "How End the Panic in Radio-TV?" (*Commentary*, October, 1952), "The known facts are few." This is true despite the appearance of a sizable book dealing with the subject, *The Judges and the Judged*, written by Merle Miller at the request of the ACLU. Its force is considerable, but it is weakened by a number of considerations, of which far and away the most important is the anonymity of Mr. Miller's principal sources of information. This he explains in a statement which is in itself an indictment of our times and a testimony to our widespread lack of courage: "The investigator felt that mentioning any name, no matter how favorable the context, might affect a livelihood now or in the future." To my knowledge, writers and actors, like some teachers, will not fight because they fear that to give battle will only complete their defeat.

In discussing what should have been done (in Chapter V), I said that writers and actors can and should be judged on the basis of particular performances. In real life, however, no "liberal" is so indifferent to personality that, given any sort of choice, he would employ a screen or radio writer or actor who was a militant Ku Kluxer or a preacher of racial

hatred. We wouldn't hire Gerald L. K. Smith to deliver
the Gettysburg Address at a public meeting.

Moreover, one must remember that the people who
pay for expensive radio and television shows want to sell
goods, and that the easiest way to sell goods is—usually—
to avoid the use of controversial subjects or personalities.
I never sought to make my living in radio-TV. As a public
figure with no great mass political following, I have been
well treated, as a rule, by the networks and independent
stations. On two or three occasions someone on the fringes
of the industry has proposed to put me on a regular "show,"
not alone—a prominent socialist could hardly expect that
—but on some form of panel discussion of important issues.
A man very high in the industry told me bluntly and hon-
estly: "No matter how good you may prove to be, no big
advertiser will buy a show in which so prominent a socialist
as you plays a leading part, and no network will undertake
a program indefinitely which cannot be sold." Twice, at
intervals, the "owner" of a popular program, not dealing
with politics or economics, approached me with a tenta-
tive invitation to be a guest on it. Both times he withdrew
the invitation at the request or in fear of the sponsor.

That, I admit, is not blacklisting in the sense in which
actors like Jean Muir or Philip Loeb seem to have been
blacklisted. Their politics had no logical relation to their
professional roles. But it illustrates the difficulty of pro-
nouncing judgment on the employers of talent as long as

their main business is to sell goods to a public in no militant mood for defending Jeffersonian principles.

The best we can do is to cultivate among employers, and in the public mind, the conviction that it is utterly unfair to damn a writer or actor to the hell of unemployment on the basis of his occasional aid to organizations and causes now listed as communist in control or sympathy. The listing isn't always correct; the contact of the artist with the organization which is listed may have been slight, based on faulty information, or remote in time. In principle we can and should judge the particular performance rather than the personal convictions of the man. Insofar as the artist's actions as a citizen enter into the public's judgments or the decisions of a prospective employer, a vital question concerns the time of these actions. Most of us, including artists, have a capacity for learning from past mistakes, over which we should not be expected publicly to beat our breasts. And all of us, most of all the artists, can be stifled in the atmosphere of enforced conformity.

That is why it was so lamentable that many writers and artists fell to a considerable degree under the spell of communism while it was easy to be fellow travelers. In fellow-traveling, they never learned the tolerance and breadth of understanding that now are denied by McCarthyism. (Are not communism and McCarthyism sisters under the skin in respect to intolerance?)

Mr. Berg in the article to which I have referred makes

a case for a "fair-minded board of inquiry such as has been proposed by management and trade union officials alike to pass on charges of present sympathy with subversive communism." I find his argument and his practical answer to certain fairly obvious objections rather persuasive. Such a board, however, would be effective only to the extent that it might inform the public and help to educate it out of its current tendency to confuse heresy with conspiracy.

XII.

The Future of Freedom

REFLECTION ON THE RECORD which has been examined here scarcely warrants hysterical charges at home and abroad that America is already given over to an anticommunist hysteria which has all but destroyed the liberties of her citizens. We are not helped in fighting evil by exaggerating its extent. In rejecting or refuting the exaggeration, men often make the truth a victim. The labor unions greatly weakened their sound case against the Taft-Hartley Act by calling it a slave-labor bill. If the foes of freedom are strong, so are the forces enlisted in its support. It is no time to cry out that "the struggle naught availeth."

But the situation is serious and the trend as I write is still in the wrong direction. We cannot continue it without risking the tragic fate of losing to our enemy by imitating him in the very contempt for freedom which first aroused our fears.

The danger of the hour is magnified by the effect of McCarthyism on public opinion abroad, the same public opinion on which we must depend for support in the cold war. Senator McCarthy himself here and abroad has become in exaggerated degree either a hero or a bogeyman—a figure half of wrath, half of contempt. We have long been aware how greatly our race discrimination is magnified and played up against us. Today our beloved country is also judged by the execution of the Rosenbergs, by convictions under the Smith Act, by exclusion of alien visitors and immigrants under the McCarran-Walter Act. And in that judgment, she is gravely discredited as the guardian and champion of all men's freedom.

Against this judgment, thoughtful Americans can, indeed, make a strong plea in mitigation and defense. We can point out how real are the freedoms we enjoy in themselves and in contrast to the despotism of communist and fascist regimes. We can, if we will, challenge our fellow democracies, like ourselves imperfectly loyal to the faith we profess, in the familiar words: "He that is without sin among you, let him first cast a stone." In many lands, our voice will be almost drowned out in the din of communist and anti-American propaganda. It will fall on ears more or less dulled by conscious and unconscious jealousy of America, resentment of our power, of our position of leadership, even of our beneficence.

I wrote the first draft of this chapter on the morning

of June 16, 1953. Before me lay a morning paper which told me that some books in our information centers abroad "were literally burned after inquiry," and that once more the Supreme Court refused to review the Rosenberg case or to grant a stay. The same paper told me that a check of public libraries in thirty cities showed communist books in use without restrictions; that the high court, true to a reasonable statute of limitations, freed Harry Bridges, convicted of perjury for denying he was a communist when he applied for naturalization; and that it barred a civil suit for damages brought to enforce a covenant embodying racial restrictions on the sale or lease of property. As I read this news, I was sure that thousands of Asians and Europeans would learn the first set of facts (often in distorted form) for every one who learned the second. Later on, a trip to Europe and North Africa more than confirmed those fears.

Only to a small degree does the remedy lie in improving our propaganda. That ought to be done. It cannot be done by a Voice of America all but ruined by McCarthyist attacks and false economies. It cannot be done at all if our deeds give the lie to our professed love of freedom.

Hitherto so fantastic were the Russian communist denials of decent right that by comparison even a McCarthyist America looked like a refuge for freedom. But during the months that I have been working on this book, the Kremlin has had the sense to modify or repeal restrictions which in its own interest it never should have imposed. So great were the Russian abominations that these concessions, normally scarcely to be noticed, have excessively impressed much of the world—but not the people of East Germany—as harbingers of a new spirit in communism. It is doubtful if there is any basic change in the communist drive for universal power. But in dealing with the new feeling about Russia and communism in the West, the American government will need all its powers of reason and a genuine regard for human freedom. It enters this new phase terribly handicapped by the burden of McCarthyism.

At the worst, evolution in Russia toward reasonableness, and in America toward McCarthyism, would tend to reduce the cold war to that which it has not been—principally a power conflict between mighty nations, both of them, in varying degree, police states, a conflict sooner or later likely to drench the earth in blood. At best the evolution might make for an uneasy coexistence of two nations both of which reject wholly or in large part the Jeffersonian dream—the dream that free men in fellowship may conquer war and poverty. Partially, we Americans carried over the dream from the agrarian society beloved by Jefferson, and we were fulfilling it in our complex industrial economy. Now it has become the world's one best hope. Should it fail, the lights of peace and freedom will indeed go out all over the world.

Longer ago than I like to remember I had to learn the

closing stanzas of Longfellow's "The Building of the Ship,"
for Friday speakin' in public school. The familiar last stanza
begins:

> Thou, too, sail on, O Ship of State!
> Sail on, O Union, strong and great!
> Humanity with all its fears,
> With all the hopes of future years,
> Is hanging breathless on thy fate!

Not great poetry, but nevertheless a sober statement
of truth. To us Americans much has been given; of us much
is required. With all our faults and mistakes, it is our
strength in support of the freedom our forefathers loved
which has saved mankind from subjection to totalitarian
power. If we now fail, the vision will perish, not soon to be
revived. It is for us to prove that neither communism nor
McCarthyism is the end of the American dream.

The Bill of Rights

Articles I–X of Amendment to the
Constitution of the United States,
in effect November 3, 1791.

ARTICLE I

Congress shall make no law respecting an establishment of religion, or prohibiting the free exercise thereof;
or abridging the freedom of speech, or of the press; or the
right of the people peaceably to assemble, and to petition
the Government for a redress of grievances.

ARTICLE II

A well regulated Militia, being necessary to the security of a free State, the right of the people to keep and bear
Arms, shall not be infringed.

ARTICLE III

No Soldier shall, in time of peace be quartered in any house, without the consent of the Owner, nor in time of war, but in a manner to be prescribed by law.

ARTICLE IV

The right of the people to be secure in their persons, houses, papers, and effects, against unreasonable searches and seizures, shall not be violated, and no Warrants shall issue, but upon probable cause, supported by Oath or affirmation, and particularly describing the place to be searched, and the persons or things to be seized.

ARTICLE V

No person shall be held to answer for a capital, or otherwise infamous crime, unless on a presentment or indictment of a Grand Jury, except in cases arising in the land or naval forces, or in the Militia, when in actual service in time of War or public danger; nor shall any person be subject for the same offence to be twice put in jeopardy of life or limb; nor shall be compelled in any criminal case to be a witness against himself, nor be deprived of life, liberty, or property, without due process of law; nor shall private property be taken for public use, without just compensation.

ARTICLE VI

In all criminal prosecutions, the accused shall enjoy the right to a speedy and public trial, by an impartial jury of the State and district wherein the crime shall have been committed, which district shall have been previously ascertained by law, and to be informed of the nature and cause of the accusation; to be confronted with the witnesses against him; to have compulsory process for obtaining witnesses in his favor, and to have the Assistance of Counsel for his defence.

ARTICLE VII

In Suits at common law, where the value in controversy shall exceed twenty dollars, the right of trial by jury shall be preserved, and no fact tried by a jury, shall be otherwise re-examined in any Court of the United States, than according to the rules of the common law.

ARTICLE VIII

Excessive bail shall not be required, nor excessive fines imposed, nor cruel and unusual punishments inflicted.

ARTICLE IX

The enumeration in the Constitution, of certain rights,

shall not be construed to deny or disparage others retained by the people.

ARTICLE X

The powers not delegated to the United States by the Constitution, nor prohibited by it to the States, are reserved to the States respectively, or to the people.

Index